# PRAYERS
# FOR
# UNCERTAIN
# TIMES

JoAnne Simmons

# PRAYERS FOR UNCERTAIN TIMES

When You Don't Know What to Pray

BARBOUR
PUBLISHING

Print ISBN 978-1-63609-482-3

Published by Barbour Publishing, Inc., 1810 Barbour Drive, Uhrichsville, Ohio 44683, www.barbourbooks.com

*Our mission is to inspire the world with the life-changing message of the Bible.*

Member of the
Evangelical Christian
Publishers Association

# CONTENTS

# INTRODUCTION

*Rejoice always, pray without ceasing, give
thanks in all circumstances; for this is the
will of God in Christ Jesus for you.*
1 Thessalonians 5:16–18 esv

"Pray without ceasing," God's Word tells us. We too easily forget that instruction sometimes, especially when we're feeling confident and sure. But in uncertain times, we're usually more aware of our reliance on God. And therein lies a blessing, no matter the questions and challenges and insecurities of life. Although we might not always know how to talk to God in uncertain times, we definitely realize our desperate need to do so. And while prayer is no magic solution that always fixes and removes a problem, it does draw us closer to the one who has and *is* the solution. He may or may not answer in the ways we want, but He will support and sustain us in the ways that we need—and in the ways that work together to accomplish His perfect plans.

May the prayers in this book ignite a deeper conversation and inspire a closer relationship with your heavenly Father, one who loves you dearly. He's the one who wants to comfort and carry you through every uncertain time.

# ANXIETY

*The Lord is near. Do not be anxious about anything, but in every situation, by prayer and petition, with thanksgiving, present your requests to God. And the peace of God. . .will guard your hearts and your minds in Christ Jesus.*
PHILIPPIANS 4:5–7 NIV

---

Anxiety—feelings of dread, fear, and uneasiness around impending or anticipated troubles—can consume our minds, which can then trigger stressors that take their physical toll on our bodies, even to the point of causing heart-racing panic. During such attacks, grounding exercises can help us escape the spiral of anxious thoughts. We can ground ourselves by observing what we're experiencing in the moment and then focusing on those observations with our five senses: What are the things we can we see, hear, feel, smell, and taste? And as Christians, we can go one better by adding gratitude to the grounding exercises, asking ourselves, *What can I thank God for?*

When anxiety feels overwhelming, we can choose to thank God for the blessings we're observing and sensing in the moment—even if they're simply the ability to take a deep breath or the opportunity to feel sunshine on our faces. Then we can focus on the truth that God our Creator and Provider is always near, ready to give us His peace beyond our understanding.

**LORD**, it feels impossible to never be anxious about anything, so I'm glad nothing is impossible for You! When I feel anxiety overwhelming me, please ground me in Your goodness. Help me focus intentionally on specific blessings surrounding me. I choose to rejoice in You with praise and gratitude, despite my circumstances, as You fill me with Your incredible, unexplainable peace.

**DEAR GOD**, please help me to fix my thoughts on what is "true, and honorable, and right, and pure, and lovely, and admirable." Help me "think about things that are excellent and worthy of praise" (Philippians 4:8 NLT). You are the God of peace, and I believe You are with me.

**DEAR LORD,** I want to seek and pursue peace (Psalm 34:14). Please show me anything that I'm doing that is hindering Your calm within me. Reveal to me what choices I'm making, what bad habits I'm entertaining, or what sin I'm holding on to that's fostering anxiety in my mind and body and keeping me captive.

**FATHER,** thank You for sending the Holy Spirit, my Helper, to live within me and be my Advocate and Intercessor before You (John 14:26). I trust that when I feel so anxious and confused that I don't even know what to pray, the Spirit is praying for me, interpreting what I cannot put into words. Whatever is happening in my life, Lord, I trust that You are working all things together for the good of I who loves You (Romans 8:26–28).

**LORD**, I'm afraid! It feels like my anxious thoughts and racing heart will never, ever stop. Please help me to focus on deep breaths and the tangible blessings I'm experiencing in this moment. Fill my mind with Your goodness and the truth of Your Word. Help me to impress upon my mind that You "keep in perfect peace all who trust in You, all whose thoughts are fixed on You" (Isaiah 26:3 NLT).

**FATHER**, please give me the wisdom and humility to know when I need help from others for my ongoing anxiety. Lead me to the right people who can guide me in both sound and studied mental health care practices and, even more importantly, in the wisdom and truth of Your Word.

**LORD OF PEACE**, Your Word tells me to cast all my cares on You (1 Peter 5:7)! In this moment, I am picturing myself taking hold of my anxious thoughts and throwing them at You to catch and destroy. Thank You for taking the burden of them away from me. Help me to trust in Your constant loving care.

**FATHER**, You tell those with an anxious heart to "Be strong, and do not fear, for your God is coming to destroy your enemies. He is coming to save you" (Isaiah 35:4 NLT). I believe those words are for me to learn from today. Help me to be strong and brave in the midst of this anxiety. For I know, I believe, You will rescue me!

**HEAVENLY FATHER**, "when my worry is great within me, Your comfort brings joy to my soul" (Psalm 94:19 NLV). Thank You!

Anxiety in my heart sure is weighing me down, Lord, so please lift me up with good words (Proverbs 12:25). Speak to my heart and mind. Lead me to the scriptures I especially need right now. Encourage my family and friends to say the words You want me to hear, words that will uplift me. Let the songs on the radio and in my playlists put my focus on You and fill me with praise. Thank You for showing me Your love and care in these ways.

**JESUS**, please let Your peace rule in my heart (Colossians 3:15) today and every day.

**DEAR JESUS**, I can almost hear You say, "You are anxious and troubled about many things, but one thing is necessary" (Luke 10:41–42 ESV). Help me, Lord, to choose that one thing needful: to sit at Your feet to listen and learn from You and simply enjoy Your presence. Help me to stop this needless fretting and fussing and just rest and relax in Your presence and Word.

**GOD**, You are the Lord of peace! I believe that with all of my heart. Please give me peace at all times in every way (2 Thessalonians 3:16).

# ASKING FOR FORGIVENESS

*He does not punish us for all our sins; he does not deal
harshly with us, as we deserve. For his unfailing love
toward those who fear him is as great as the height
of the heavens above the earth. He has removed
our sins as far from us as the east is from the west.
The LORD is like a father to his children, tender
and compassionate to those who fear him.*

PSALM 103:10–13 NLT

When we've made a mistake and have done everything we can to try to correct the wrong or restore
the relationship by asking forgiveness from those
our mistake has affected, then we've done all we can
do. The ball is no longer in our court. Yet the uncertainty of whether our offenses will be held against
us or we'll be given grace can be excruciating. While
there is no guarantee amid societal rules and human
relationships that we will be forgiven, God promises
His grace: "If we confess our sins, he is faithful and
just and will forgive us our sins and purify us from
all unrighteousness" (1 John 1:9 NIV). We can hope
and pray for people to give grace when we need it,
but even if they do not, God's grace is never-ending
and always amazing.

**LORD**, I'm so worried I won't be forgiven in this circumstance. You know my heart and that I am truly, deeply sorry for what I've done. So regardless of what happens in this earthly world, help me have peace knowing that because I have confessed my sin before You, You, Lord of heaven, have removed it as far as the east is from the west (Psalm 103:12). And that's what matters most. Although I long for this circumstance to be resolved with grace and forgiveness and reconciliation from those I've hurt, I will rest in and trust in Your grace and forgiveness for me.

You are the example we all should follow in forgiveness, Father. May all people "be kind to one another, tenderhearted, forgiving one another" (Ephesians 4:32 ESV) as You have forgiven us through Christ.

**HEAVENLY FATHER**, I know Your Word warns that if I don't forgive others, then You won't forgive me (Matthew 6:14–15). And I shouldn't expect others to show me mercy if I do not show mercy (Luke 6:36) to others as well. So as I wait and hope for forgiveness in this uncertain time, please show me any areas where I need to extend mercy and offer forgiveness. Has there been an offense I've been holding against someone? Please help me to let go of it and make things right where I can.

**DEAR JESUS**, please help me to fully understand and apply what You meant when You said, "Not seven times but seventy times seven" (Matthew 18:22 NLV) when it comes to forgiveness. I want to be full of mercy for others just like You are.

# BETRAYAL

*Jesus was troubled in his spirit, and testified,*
*"Truly, truly, I say to you, one of you will betray me."*
JOHN 13:21 ESV

Jesus, our sinless Savior, did nothing to deserve the brutal betrayal He received from His former friend and follower Judas. Nor did He deserve Peter's denials of even knowing Him! So Jesus can surely relate when we suffer through betrayal as well. We are blessed to have a Savior who was "made in every respect like us, his brothers and sisters, so that he could be our merciful and faithful High Priest before God" (Hebrews 2:17 NLT) and who "understands our weaknesses, for he faced all of the same testings we do" (Hebrews 4:15 NLT). If you are suffering through a betrayal, cry out to Jesus who knows and understands. Let Him comfort and assure you that God will "never leave you nor forsake you" (Hebrews 13:5 ESV).

**JESUS**, I don't deserve this awful betrayal! Why is this happening? What did You feel like when Your friends were betraying You? I know Your Word says Your Spirit was troubled by Judas's actions (John 13:21). And I'm sure Peter's denials disappointed You. Yet I'm grateful You can relate to what I'm now experiencing. Please help me to remember that through the betrayals You endured, the Father was working out His plan to offer salvation to all people. I pray that You will somehow make good come from this betrayal I am suffering too, trusting Your promise to do so is true (Romans 8:28).

The psalmist prayed, "Even my best friend, the one I trusted completely, the one who shared my food, has turned against me" (Psalm 41:9 NLT), and I am praying that too today, God! This betrayal hurts so bad and makes me so angry! Please, Lord, help me to have self-control and wisdom. Help me to trust that You are working to bring justice to this situation.

**DEAR GOD**, I know exactly the pain the psalmist is describing when he writes, "It is not an enemy who taunts me—I could bear that. It is not my foes who so arrogantly insult me—I could have hidden from them. Instead, it is you—my equal, my companion and close friend. What good fellowship we once enjoyed as we walked together to the house of God" (Psalm 55:12–14 NLT). I, too, feel so betrayed right now by my equal, my companion, my close friend. Please draw me closer to You and teach me what You want me to learn through this experience, God. Please comfort and heal my broken heart.

**DEAR LORD**, my betrayer sure feels like an enemy, yet I know You have said to love my enemies and pray for them (Matthew 5:44). I need Your supernatural help with that, please. I cannot do it without You.

"I give praise to You, O God. Do not be quiet. For sinners and liars have opened their mouths against me. They have spoken against me with lying tongues. They have gathered around me with words of hate. They fought against me for no reason. I give them my love but they speak against me in return. But I am in prayer. They pay me what is bad for what is good. They give me hate for my love" (Psalm 109:1–5 NLV).

**FATHER**, when I read the story of Samson and Delilah, I see how Delilah betrayed Samson. And I also see how Samson was very disobedient to You during his life. Because of that, he put himself into bad situations that brought a lot of negative consequences down upon him. Help me, Lord, to learn from Samson's life and mistakes. Help me to see how You can and do accomplish Your perfect plans in all kinds of ways, through all kinds of people.

"I come to you for protection, O Lord my God. Save me from my persecutors—rescue me! If you don't, they will maul me like a lion, tearing me to pieces with no one to rescue me. O Lord my God, if I have done wrong or am guilty of injustice, if I have betrayed a friend or plundered my enemy without cause, then let my enemies capture me" (Psalm 7:1–5 NLT).

**DEAR GOD**, Your Word warns me in 2 Timothy 3:3–5 (NLT) about people in the last days, saying, "They will be unloving and unforgiving; they will slander others and have no self-control. They will be cruel and hate what is good. They will betray their friends, be reckless, be puffed up with pride, and love pleasure rather than God. They will act religious, but they will reject the power that could make them godly." Please, God, help me to "stay away from people like that!"

**DEAR JESUS**, as Judas betrayed You with a kiss, You said, "Friend, do what you came to do" (Matthew 26:50 ESV). I don't know that I could ever be so calm and practice such self-control in such an outrageous situation. I am in awe of You, my perfect, sinless Savior. Please help me to be more like You!

"Even a friend of mine whom I trusted, who ate my bread, has turned against me. Have loving-kindness for me, O Lord. Raise me up, so that I may pay them back. Then I will know that You are pleased with me, because he who hates me does not win over me. As for me, You hold me up in my honesty. And You set me beside You forever. Honor be to the Lord, the God of Israel, forever and ever! Let it be so!" (Psalm 41:9–13 NLV).

# BROKEN RELATIONSHIPS

*Now from the sixth hour there was darkness over all the land until the ninth hour. And about the ninth hour Jesus cried out with a loud voice, saying, "Eli, Eli, lema sabachthani?" that is, "My God, my God, why have you forsaken me?*
MATTHEW 27:45–46 ESV

Whether we know a relationship needed to end or we are blindsided and devastated by the loss, broken relationships bring a unique kind of pain and grief. And in that pain and grief, there is no one better to turn to than Jesus Christ our Savior. He felt the worst kind of broken relationship when He hung on the cross and the Father had to turn away from Him because He could not look up on the sin that our perfect Savior took upon Himself to pay its penalty for us. In the midst of the pain and uncertainty of any broken relationship you might be experiencing, stay close to Jesus. He knows your hurt and suffering. Let Him empathize with you, comfort you, and encourage you.

This relationship feels broken beyond repair, God! Yet You can restore anything. Show me a miracle, please.

**HEAVENLY FATHER**, I am so hurt and confused. Please give me wisdom to know if the ending of this relationship will ultimately be a good thing, or if I need to seek to mend and restore it. Either way, help me not to sin in this difficult situation. If I have erred in Your eyes, show me as I ask for Your forgiveness. And as I move forward, guide my words and my actions.

**LORD**, speak Your wisdom and compassion to us through loved ones, friends, mentors, and counselors as we navigate this broken relationship. Soften our hearts and let us be willing to listen well.

When people let me down and disappoint me, Lord, help me to remember that You never, ever will. You are right and good in all Your ways, and kind in all Your works (Psalm 145:17).

**FATHER**, forgive me for my part in this broken relationship. Thank You for Your grace through Jesus Christ my Savior.

**JESUS**, when I feel abandoned, remind me that Paul felt Your presence and strength when he needed support and everyone but You abandoned him. He wrote, "At my first defense, no one came to my support, but everyone deserted me. May it not be held against them. But the Lord stood at my side and gave me strength" (2 Timothy 4:16–17 NIV). When I feel alone, abandoned, deserted, remind me that You are standing right by my side, giving me strength.

**LORD**, please help us to "get rid of all bitterness, rage, anger, harsh words, and slander, as well as all types of evil behavior" and to be "kind to each another, tenderhearted, forgiving one another" as You forgave us through Christ (Ephesians 4:31–32 NLT). And whatever the outcome of this broken relationship, please help me to "strive for peace with everyone" (Hebrews 12:14 ESV).

**FATHER**, remind me that I cannot change or control other people. I can only control my own thoughts and words and actions and behaviors. Please help me to do so in ways that keep me from sin and that bring honor and glory to You.

# CHILDREN

*Children are a gift from the LORD; they are a reward from him. Children born to a young man are like arrows in a warrior's hands. How joyful is the man whose quiver is full of them!*
PSALM 127:3–5 NLT

Children certainly are a blessing—and a source of great uncertainty. Even the most involved and observant parents who feel they can predict their child's behavior in great detail can't deny the curveballs kids can expertly throw. God has given them free will, just like He has given it to us all—and with every new age and stage of our children, we must adapt and be intentional if we want to correct, guide, and nurture well. To be wise and intentional parents, then, we must be in constant prayer as we seek God's wisdom and guidance.

**FATHER**, You are the very best parent of all. You are my mentor and role model. Help me to love and guide my children like You love and guide me and all Your other children. I want to hunger for Your instruction through Your Word. Parenting is the most important job ever, and I cannot do this well without You.

**LORD**, help me to study and remember wisdom from the Proverbs as I parent. Your Word says, "Discipline your children, and they will give you peace of mind and will make your heart glad" (Proverbs 29:17 NLT). Give me the strength to right my children when they go down the wrong road, knowing You will be with me as I do so.

**LORD,** I want to train my children in the ways they should go so that even when they are old, they will not depart from it (Proverbs 22:6). Please cover my parenting mistakes with Your grace. Show me how to correct my mistakes even as I help my children correct their own.

**DEAR GOD,** I have to admit—my children are driving me absolutely nuts in this situation right now. You know I love them dearly. Yet You also know how much I need Your help to control my anger and frustration. I beg You to bless me with Your supernatural love and joy and peace and patience and kindness and goodness and faithfulness and gentleness and self-control!

**FATHER**, I feel so stressed! I am trying to do everything right in this situation with my child, yet nothing seems to be improving. Keep me calm and steady. Help me to stay the course with Your wisdom and grace.

**JESUS**, when the disciples tried to keep little children away from You, You became angry! You said, "Let the children come to me. Don't stop them! For the Kingdom of God belongs to those who are like these children. I tell you the truth, anyone who doesn't receive the Kingdom of God like a child will never enter it" (Mark 10:14–15 NLT), and then You took the children in Your arms, placed Your hands on their heads, and blessed them. Remind me every day how You love children and how important they are.

**FATHER**, help me to teach my children to not just obey me because I am their mom but because obeying in general is important. It's the right thing to do. For Your Word says in Ephesians 6:1–3 (ESV), "Children, obey your parents in the Lord, for this is right. 'Honor your father and mother' (this is the first commandment with a promise), 'that it may go well with you and that you may live long in the land.'"

**JESUS**, You said, "See that you do not despise one of these little ones. For I tell you that in heaven their angels always see the face of my Father who is in heaven" (Matthew 18:10 ESV). Lord, may these words help me to treasure and value children like You do!

Fill in all the gaps, God. I know I fall short and make mistakes every single day as I try to parent with wisdom and love. Because of my shortcomings, I pray You will help my children see their need to look to You as the best parent of all. Remind me that I can never be all they need—no person can!—but You can and are! All their purpose and fulfillment are found in You, our Lord and Creator!

**LORD**, it amazes me that although I love my kids beyond words, You love them even more. And for that I thank and praise You!

My children are always ultimately Yours, Father! Thank You for entrusting them to me as their earthly parent. They are such a gift and blessing. I praise You for the joy and responsibility of them. Help me never take that for granted.

For them to live this life for You, God, my kids need to know Your Word and be able to read, study, and apply it. I cannot teach them well unless I myself am regularly learning from and being corrected by Your Word. Thus, I pray You would create an endless, never-fully-satisfied hunger for Your Word in our family.

**FATHER**, fellowship with other believers is a vital part of my parenting. To that end, I pray You would help us to be a family that loves Your church, the body of believers, and that loves serving and growing and being part of a family of believers in a local Bible-teaching church.

I fear for my kids' safety and well-being too much, God. Sometimes it fills me with so much anxiety. They are so small and helpless and in need of such care. As my children grow and mature, some of my fears and anxious thoughts may dissipate as they become more capable and independent—but then new fears and anxieties rise up to take the place of the old ones. Oh, Lord, how I need Your peace. Remind me that You are sovereign and in control, and I am not. That my children are in Your hands, from beginning to end.

**LORD**, please show me the parents from whom I can learn. Help me to build strong friendships with older, wiser moms and dads who also follow You, so that they can speak lovingly, honestly, and boldly into my life to help encourage me and correct me in my parenting.

**JESUS**, there is nothing more important in raising my children than helping lead them to You as Savior. Help me to point them to the gospel in everything I do. Help me to teach them about what sin is and that You are the only solution for the missteps of each person. Thank You for dying for sin and rising again, for offering the gift of grace to anyone who accepts You as Savior!

**FATHER**, help me to instill in my children the truth from Your Word that they are Your handiwork. That they are uniquely created in Christ Jesus to do good works, which You prepared in advance for them to do (Ephesians 2:10).

**DEAR GOD**, help my children listen to fatherly correction and motherly instruction (Proverbs 1:8). Help them realize how much we as parents want Your best for them.

**LORD**, as I raise my children, I don't want to provoke them to anger by the way I treat them. Help me to bring them up with the discipline and instruction that comes from You (Ephesians 6:4).

My kids often humble me, Lord, and that's a good thing. I pray You would keep me humble always—and if that means apologizing to them when necessary, and making amends where needed, I pray You would give me the strength to do so.

# CHRONIC PAIN/ILLNESS

*He will wipe away every tear from their eyes,*
*and death shall be no more, neither shall there*
*be mourning, nor crying, nor pain anymore,*
*for the former things have passed away."*

REVELATION 21:4 ESV

---

Our ultimate hope for an end to chronic pain and illness is heaven where there will be no more of either. But meanwhile, here on earth, if we are suffering we can ask God to help us endure, to give us His strength, and to show us His purposes, knowing that the suffering we're enduring now is nothing compared with the glory that will be revealed in us later (Romans 8:18). Even when we don't understand how or why, we can trust that God is working good through our circumstances as we remain faithful to Him. We can even rejoice knowing that "suffering produces endurance, and endurance produces character, and character produces hope" (Romans 5:3–4 ESV).

**JESUS**, I long for Your presence and Your healing touch. Oh, that I could feel Your hand upon me and experience a miracle! When You lived here on earth, You touched and healed all kinds of people with all kinds of ailments for nothing is impossible with You. I know Your presence is here with me now through the Holy Spirit. If it is Your will, please take this disease from me like only You can.

**FATHER**, I believe Your Word that says, "The LORD nurses them when they are sick and restores them to health" (Psalm 41:3 NLT). Be my nurse, my loving care, Lord! Please restore my health in whatever way seems good to You.

**GOD**, will I ever feel normal and well again, or is this my new normal? Will I ever be healed from this pain and affliction? I know I will be in heaven someday, but will I be healed here on earth? I believe wholeheartedly that You have all power to heal me. I know my will is to be healed right this very moment, but I want *Your* will most of all. Please strengthen and sustain me as I live this life Your way, in Your presence.

**LORD**, teach me what You want me to learn through this illness, this condition. I believe that in all things You want me to become more like Christ. He suffered on this earth, and in my suffering, I share in His, drawing ever closer in relationship to my Savior, my strength, my refuge.

**GOD**, I believe that "a joyful heart is good medicine, but a crushed spirit dries up the bones" (Proverbs 17:22 ESV). Even while I struggle with this illness, please keep my heart full of joy. Fill me up with gratitude as I focus on all my blessings, on all the things that are right and worthy to be thought of. Help me to have a good sense of humor and notice all reasons to smile and laugh, to rejoice in You.

**LORD**, Your Word says, "Is anyone among you sick? Let him call for the elders of the church, and let them pray over him, anointing him with oil in the name of the Lord" (James 5:14 ESV). Give me the humility to ask others for prayer and to thank those in my church and elsewhere who already pray for me and care for me.

**HEAVENLY FATHER**, some days this pain and illness discourage me so much that I fear my going into a deep depression. Lift me up out of the darkness and into Your light! Even when I don't understand my circumstances, help me to keep faith and have joy in You!

**DEAR GOD**, You know my heart and thoughts. You know I struggle with anger over this endless-seeming pain and illness. I don't understand why You don't heal me right now and take this all away from me. I want to be healthy and whole again. But more than that, I want to live in Your will and way. So in this moment, I confess my anger to You. I know You love me more than I could ever know. Thus, I trust that as I struggle with my frustration and questioning, You will continue to help me work my way through it, drawing me ever closer to You in the process.

**LORD**, I feel like I'm wearing out, so help me to focus on not giving up. Show me how my spirit is getting stronger every day. I believe this truth from Your Word: "This is the reason we do not give up. Our human body is wearing out. But our spirits are getting stronger every day. The little troubles we suffer now for a short time are making us ready for the great things God is going to give us forever. We do not look at the things that can be seen. We look at the things that cannot be seen. The things that can be seen will come to an end. But the things that cannot be seen will last forever" (2 Corinthians 4:16–18 NLV).

**LORD**, please help my loved one who is going through chronic illness. I wish I could bear some of the burden for her. Please show me the best ways and times to help, such as cooking her meals, cleaning her house, and driving her or accompanying her to doctor's appointments. Give my friend the ability to communicate with me about how I can help.

**LORD**, when it's my child or spouse going through chronic illness and pain, I can barely stand it. I love them so much and I hate to see them struggle. I'd rather bear their suffering myself. But You are sovereign, and You have kept me well so that I can be strong for them and encourage them. So please strengthen me like only You can. Encourage me with Your love and care so that I can pass it on.

# CHURCH CONFLICT

*You are citizens together with those who belong to God. You belong in God's family. This family is built on the teachings of the missionaries and the early preachers. Jesus Christ Himself is the cornerstone, which is the most important part of the building. Christ keeps this building together and it is growing into a holy building for the Lord. You are also being put together as a part of this building because God lives in you by His Spirit.*

Ephesians 2:19–22 NLV

In any local church we attend, get involved with, or become a member in, we will observe and experience conflict. No person is perfect, and so of course a local church made up of imperfect people cannot be perfect either. When we become part of a church community with that reality in mind, we won't be devastated when church conflict happens. Instead, we can focus on being a family of believers who want to be in community, who desire to learn about and fellowship and worship God together. We can realize that conflict is a part of life that must be acknowledged and worked through with love and grace.

**LORD**, give me wisdom to know what issues need to be worked through in my church and what ones are just not worth arguing about, such as the little, petty things and minor differences of opinion that should just roll off our backs. Help us all be easygoing and full of wisdom, grace, compassion, and forgiveness toward one another. Help us to be merciful to each other, just as You are merciful to us.

**FATHER**, help the members of my church family to never be quick in our spirits to become angry. Help us to remember that "anger lodges in the heart of fools" (Ecclesiastes 7:9 ESV). When we do have anger, help us to communicate well about it and resolve it quickly.

Please guide the pastors and leaders of my church, Lord. Help them to love Your Word, to follow it and teach it well. Help them to wisely deal with the attacks that come upon them. Fill them with Your supernatural strength and compassion so that they can lead and shepherd in the ways that honor You and further Your kingdom.

**GOD**, I pray that we who attend our church can focus on letting the Word of Christ dwell in us richly as we teach and admonish one another in all wisdom, singing psalms and hymns and spiritual songs, with thankfulness to You in our hearts (Colossians 3:16).

**DEAR GOD**, may my church family do its best to consider how to stir up one another to love and good works. May we not neglect to meet together, as is the habit of some, but encourage one another, all the more as we see the day of Your Son's return drawing near (Hebrews 10:24–25).

**FATHER**, please help Your church focus on the simplicity and effectiveness of continuing "stedfastly in the apostles' doctrine and fellowship, and in breaking of bread, and in prayers" (Acts 2:42 KJV).

**GOD**, thank You for Your instruction through Paul in Romans 12. Help us to follow it. Help us to remember that "just as our bodies have many parts and each part has a special function, so it is with Christ's body. We are many parts of one body, and we all belong to each other" (Romans 12:4–5 NLT).

**FATHER**, forgive us for our sins, flaws, failures, and fights. Help us build up our faith and fidelity to You. And even though the church is not perfect, please keep adding to our numbers all over the world, "day by day those who [are] being saved" (Acts 2:47 ESV).

**LORD**, I pray that my church leaders would watch over themselves and all the flock of which the Holy Spirit has made them overseers. I pray that they would be good shepherds of the church of God, which Your Son, Jesus, bought with His own lifeblood.

Please help my church have peace, Father! Build us up! Help us to walk in awesome fear of the Lord and in the comfort of the Holy Spirit (Acts 9:31). Help us be a light that attracts others to You.

**GOD**, remind us of the gifts You gave the church: "the apostles, the prophets, the evangelists, and the pastors and teachers. Their responsibility is to equip God's people to do his work and build up the church, the body of Christ. This will continue until we all come to such unity in our faith and knowledge of God's Son that we will be mature in the Lord, measuring up to the full and complete standard of Christ" (Ephesians 4:11–13 NLT).

**LORD**, we seek You! We seek Your strength and Your presence continually (1 Chronicles 16:11)!

**FATHER**, help us to speak the truth in love. Help us to grow up into Christ. Help the whole body to work together well, just like You intended so that it is built up in love (Ephesians 4:15–16).

# CONFUSING RELATIONSHIPS

*Cry out for insight, and ask for understanding. Search for them as you would for silver; seek them like hidden treasures. Then you will understand what it means to fear the Lord, and you will gain knowledge of God.*

PROVERBS 2:3–5 NLT

Sometimes it's not that relationships are broken. It's just that we can't seem to figure them out. Something feels off or awkward or insincere. Maybe it's a difficult situation with a coworker or manager. Maybe a friend has suddenly grown cold toward you with vague or zero reasons why. Maybe a family relationship is tense at all times. Maybe someone treats you unfairly and rudely out of the blue. Maybe someone seems too nice, and it all seems fake. In our stress and confusion, we can turn to the God who sees and knows all. He "knows the secrets of every heart" (Psalm 44:21 NLT), and He can help us have wisdom, clarity, and good communication in the relationships that puzzle and perplex us.

**GOD**, I can't figure this out. I'm so confused by this relationship. What is going on? I believe You are not a God of confusion but a God of peace (1 Corinthians 14:33). And I believe You want to help me. So I am trusting fully in You because it's clear that I can't lean on my own understanding—I have none in this situation. Please give me clarity and peace.

**HEAVENLY FATHER**, I pray that You would help me to realize if someone is out to harm me in this confusing relationship. I know the devil prowls around in all kinds of ways looking to devour me (1 Peter 5:8). So I'm praying for Your wisdom and protection as well as Your guidance and presence in this and all other areas of my life.

"Let my cry come before you, O Lord; give me understanding according to your word!" (Psalm 119:169 esv).

**JESUS,** I know people change, sometimes for better or for worse, sometimes due to circumstances or health problems or struggles totally out of their control. The thing is that those changes can affect my relationships with others—sometimes in such confusing ways. At the same time, I know sometimes *I'm* the one changing and causing confusion. Thankfully You never change. You are the same yesterday and today and forever (Hebrews 13:8). You are my constant Savior and friend.

**LORD**, You said that You "search all hearts and examine secret motives," that You "give all people their due rewards, according to what their actions deserve" (Jeremiah 17:10 NLT). Please search and examine hearts and motives in this confusing relationship I find myself in. Reveal what needs to be revealed, and reward or reprimand as You see fit.

**GOD**, I want this confusing relationship to be one where we encourage each other and build each other up (1 Thessalonians 5:11), not where we feel anxious and awkward around each other. I pray and thank You for Your peace, comfort, guidance, and help!

# CONSTANT CHANGE

*Every good and perfect gift is from above, coming down from the Father of the heavenly lights, who does not change like shifting shadows.*

JAMES 1:17 NIV

We all need a little change here and there in our lives, or imagine how dull life would be! But constant change with no stability is chaotic and stressful. Too much variety makes for too much spice in life. Yet sometimes we find ourselves in a season of constant change we cannot control, and there appears to be no end in sight. Thankfully God does not change (Malachi 3:6). He alone is our one true constant, no matter the disorder and turmoil we might be experiencing. To Him we can draw near and hold on tight when life is tossing us around.

**HEAVENLY FATHER**, it's just been feeling like too much lately—all this change. I can't seem to catch my breath from one life-altering event to another. Keep me steady and stable as I depend on You. Help me ride the waves of change.

I love You, Lord! You are my strength. You are "my rock, and my safe place, and the One Who takes me out of trouble." You are "my safe-covering, my saving strength, and my strong tower" (Psalm 18:1–2 NLV). In You I find the peace I need to keep me standing firm.

**JESUS**, I trust You are the same yesterday, today, and forever (Hebrews 13:8). I'm so grateful that no matter what unwanted changes occur in my life, You are always the same, always my loving Savior, always my guard and guide.

**FATHER GOD**, I'm thankful that You keep Your promises. I trust that You don't act like people who change their minds and perhaps even lie to me. What You say You'll do, You do. What You have spoken, You fulfill (Numbers 23:19).

**LORD**, Your Word says that although there are times that You "[wreck] the plans of the people," Your plans "stand forever. The plans of [Your] heart stand through the future of all people" (Psalm 33:10–11 NLV). This gives me a measure of comfort. For during those times when I feel like my plans are wrecked, I can trust that You had a better plan in mind all along, that You will show me what Your perfect plans are, and that You will help me walk in step with them and You.

**JESUS**, please help me to relax and go with the flow more. Help me to understand that life is full of change. Give me the strength to fully accept that reality instead of fearing and fighting it. When old plans fall apart, help me to find the blessings and joy in what is coming on the horizon.

**LORD**, as I'm getting older, I feel like I am undergoing constant changes with my health. I have new aches and pains and ailments regularly, it seems. I long for my younger years and the health and energy I had then! Help me to accept my aging body, this vessel in which You dwell, and to care for it well with wisdom and joy for the life You have given me.

**"LORD**, you have been our dwelling place in all generations. Before the mountains were brought forth, or ever you had formed the earth and the world, from everlasting to everlasting you are God" (Psalm 90:1–2 ESV). In this I find my calm and comfort.

# CURRENT EVENTS

*"Remember this and stand firm, recall it to mind,*
*you transgressors, remember the former things*
*of old; for I am God, and there is no other; I am*
*God, and there is none like me, declaring the*
*end from the beginning and from ancient times*
*things not yet done, saying, 'My counsel shall*
*stand, and I will accomplish all my purpose.'"*
ISAIAH 46:8–10 ESV

You can lose your equilibrium, as well as your sanity, by trying to keep up with current events. But if you don't, you feel uninformed and unprepared to deal with what life might throw at you. And there are so many sources for news about current events these days—newspapers and social media and TV and blogs and podcasts—so many that it's beyond overwhelming, and all of it seems conflicting. It seems nearly impossible to determine what's really true in any situation. And so we fix our eyes and minds and hearts and attention on God's power and sovereignty. He is not surprised by current events nor detached from them. He tells "from the beginning what will happen in the end" (Isaiah 46:10 NLV).

**ALMIGHTY GOD**, help me not to be anxious over all the events going on in the world. Remind me that none of them take You by surprise. That You know and You care about what's happening. Help me to stay in Your presence, to keep me coming to You in prayer, asking for Your wisdom and guidance to know my part in doing good, making a difference, and bringing You glory.

**LORD**, help me to tune out the false and over-dramatized news about current events that just creates unnecessary anxiety. Help me to hear and know what You want me to hear and know. Keep my focus on the issues, relationships, problem-solving, and good works that You want me involved in. Tell me what I can do in times such as these.

Guide Your people in these crazy days, Lord! Keep us close to You, and help us to be lights in the darkness around us. We trust in Your promises. We trust in Your salvation. Help us to share Your truth with others so that they can see the stark contrast between hoping in the futile, chaotic things of the world and hoping in You! We trust and wait for "our blessed hope, the appearing of the glory of our great God and Savior Jesus Christ" (Titus 2:13 ESV).

In these days, evil seems to be running rampant, Lord. So I pray You would help me to live not as unwise but as wise (Ephesians 5:15). Help me to make the best use of time doing the things You want me to do.

**LORD**, please help me to seek after the good things that are going on in my area and on the other side of the globe. Even if popular news sources don't cover too much about them, I know fellow Christians all over the world are doing good works in Your name, caring for others and spreading the gospel. Hallelujah! Help me find a way to share Your love and good news too!

**FATHER**, help me to find ways to stay aware of current events without losing myself among them. Help me to use that worldly knowledge to converse intelligently with those lost in sin. Show me ways to tell others about the certainty of You in such uncertain times! Help me point them to You as the one and only Way, Truth, and Life out of this sinful world.

**DEAR GOD**, please bless and encourage the Christians who find themselves in the middle of current events. Use Your Holy Spirit to work through them to accomplish Your plans and purposes in this world.

**FATHER**, please remind me that I shouldn't be too shocked by bad news in current events, for the "whole world lies in the power of the evil one" (1 John 5:19 ESV). Yet You have ultimate power above and beyond this world. For there is nothing and no one greater than You, and all Your people have nothing to fear, because we are Yours.

# DEPRESSION/ FEELING HOPELESS

*Be strong in the Lord and in his mighty power.*
*Put on all of God's armor so that you will be able to*
*stand firm against all strategies of the devil. For we*
*are not fighting against flesh-and-blood enemies,*
*but against evil rulers and authorities of the unseen*
*world, against mighty powers in this dark world,*
*and against evil spirits in the heavenly places.*

EPHESIANS 6:10–12 NLT

Feeling depressed is common and comes and goes based on all kinds of letdowns, even just cloudy skies instead of sun. But deep and lasting depression—feeling utterly hopeless day after day—can be completely debilitating, even requiring diagnosis and professional medical help. When we are feeling down, our enemy Satan wants to destroy us with his attacks and lies that we are abandoned by God, or that there is no God and no hope anywhere at all. And so we must view depression as a time of battle, during which we must let God keep us strong as we put on His armor and stand firm in our faith, even in the deepest pits of despair.

**LORD**, please remind me of the spiritual armor that I need to put on every single day. Help me to memorize and apply this scripture so that I can fight these feelings of depression and hopelessness: "Therefore, put on every piece of God's armor so you will be able to resist the enemy in the time of evil. Then after the battle you will still be standing firm. Stand your ground, putting on the belt of truth and the body armor of God's righteousness. For shoes, put on the peace that comes from the Good News so that you will be fully prepared. In addition to all of these, hold up the shield of faith to stop the fiery arrows of the devil. Put on salvation as your helmet, and take the sword of the Spirit, which is the word of God" (Ephesians 6:13–17 NLT).

**LORD**, this struggle with depression seems so up and down and unpredictable. Some days are good and others are downright terrible. Today is awful. Please put my focus back on You and back on gratitude. Help me to take good care of both my physical and mental health. Surround me with people who care about me, and let me be fully aware of their love.

**DEAR GOD**, lead me to health-care professionals who can help me deal with and heal from my depression. Please guide me to the ones who love and honor You, ones who will help me with good mental-health-care practices and with the truth of Your Word.

**JESUS**, when the walls of depression are closing in, deep down in this pit of depression, please lift me up and out. Rescue me like only You can!

**LORD,** I so relate to the psalmist when he prays: " 'O God my rock,' I cry, 'Why have you forgotten me? Why must I wander around in grief, oppressed by my enemies?' Their taunts break my bones. They scoff, 'Where is this God of yours?' Why am I discouraged? Why is my heart so sad? I will put my hope in God! I will praise him again—my Savior and my God!" (Psalm 42:9–11 NLT).

Even though I do have questions and anguish, even though I am consumed by depression and discouragement, Lord, I will put my hope in You and choose to praise You, my Savior and my God!

"Answer me quickly, O Lord! My spirit fails! Hide not your face from me, lest I be like those who go down to the pit. Let me hear in the morning of your steadfast love, for in you I trust. Make me know the way I should go, for to you I lift up my soul" (Psalm 143:7–8 ESV).

**LORD**, I don't want to be conformed to the world. It's too much of a mess! It makes me feel depressed and hopeless. So I pray You would transform me by giving me a renewed mind. I want to be able to discern Your will knowing "what is good and acceptable and perfect" (Romans 12:2 ESV).

# DIFFICULT DECISIONS

*Tune your ears to wisdom, and concentrate on understanding. Cry out for insight, and ask for understanding. Search for them as you would for silver; seek them like hidden treasures. Then you will understand what it means to fear the LORD, and you will gain knowledge of God. For the LORD grants wisdom! From his mouth come knowledge and understanding. He grants a treasure of common sense to the honest. He is a shield to those who walk with integrity. He guards the paths of the just and protects those who are faithful to him. Then you will understand what is right, just, and fair, and you will find the right way to go. For wisdom will enter your heart, and knowledge will fill you with joy. Wise choices will watch over you. Understanding will keep you safe.*

PROVERBS 2:2–11 NLT

---

Sometimes in life we find ourselves at the crossroads of a big decision. There we may stand, feeling paralyzed, totally unsure of which way to go. Yet God is there, wanting to give us the wisdom to make the right choice, to step in the right direction. He promises, when we are truly seeking after Him, to bless our desire for wisdom and understanding and to show us the best path forward.

Not making a change feels like the easier choice right now, God, yet I feel restless and unsettled about staying the course. I feel You leading me into something new. Please give me direction and clarity about exactly what this new thing is that You are calling me to.

Speak boldly and clearly into my life regarding this big decision, Lord! Lead me to the scriptures and messages You want me to hear. Let wise loved ones in my life give me good insight. I want to listen to advice and accept instruction so that I can gain wisdom (Proverbs 19:20).

**FATHER**, in all my decisions, I want to be faithful to You and follow Your Word. Help me not to do anything that would lead me away from You and into sin. Give me red flags and warnings to stay away from certain places and people that would do me harm. Direct me to make the choices that will draw me closer to You and will help mature my faith in You.

**LORD**, I'm still waiting for clarity to know Your will and see Your specific direction in this situation. But I know above all Your will is for me to always be joyful, to never stop praying, and to be thankful in all circumstances (1 Thessalonians 5:16–18). So give me patience and the right mindset as I wait on You.

**FATHER**, sometimes I just get stuck and obsess over a decision because I want to know exactly, specifically, what Your will is for my life. But maybe You are trying to tell me that either option is great; so it's just up to me to decide. As long as my choice is not disobeying You and Your Word, I don't have to get so anxious about making the perfect choice. So I pray for Your peace and the assurance that nothing I do, no decision I make can ever stop Your loving me (Romans 8:38–39).

**LORD**, remind me that Your wisdom is there for the taking. That when I ask for wisdom, You love to give it! Help me to believe that and not doubt. For I don't want to be like a wave of the sea that's blown and tossed by the wind (James 1:5–8).

**LORD,** You see the bigger picture, a view that is shielded from me right now. Yet that doesn't keep me from wanting to jump ahead and see the final results, the happy ending that will come from making this difficult decision. But You are leading me step by step and day by day. Help me to be content with that. Help me appreciate the ways You are growing my faith and making me more dependent on You.

**LORD,** please take away the anxiety that I'm feeling over this decision. Clear my head of all worry. Fill me with joy and gratitude for the fact that I have freedom and options. Help me to remember that You have all things in hand. Prompt me to thank You for all of Your blessings to me!

# DISABILITY

*As Jesus was walking along, he saw a man who had*
*been blind from birth. "Rabbi," his disciples asked*
*him, "why was this man born blind? Was it because of*
*his own sins or his parents' sins?" "It was not because*
*of his sins or his parents' sins," Jesus answered. "This*
*happened so the power of God could be seen in him."*
JOHN 9:1–3 NLT

---

Disability causes all kinds of extra uncertainty and
challenges in an already challenging and uncertain
world. And so what a blessing it is to remember the
words of Jesus regarding a disability of blindness:
"This happened so the power of God could be seen
in him." No matter how difficult and exhausting the
disabilities we might be enduring, have been enduring, and see no end in enduring until heaven, we can
choose to focus on them as opportunities to let the
power of God be seen in us—allowing opportunities
to shine His supernatural strength and peace and
promises through us to a world that so desperately
needs hope.

This disability is exhausting, Lord. Sometimes I grow so frustrated thinking how I could serve You so much better if I didn't have all these issues. So, remind me how You are using this disability for Your power to be seen in my life. I want to glorify You in any way I can!

**FATHER GOD**, help me to remember every day that "the sufferings of this present time are not worth comparing with the glory that is to be revealed" in me (Romans 8:18 ESV).

**LORD**, I am in so much physical pain with my disability today. Please relieve it in a miraculous way!

My disability makes me fear for the future, Lord. I wonder what will happen to me. But I trust that because You know every hair of my head, You surely know about my disability. Just as You know and care for the lowly sparrows, surely You will always know about and take care of me (Matthew 10:29–31).

Paul said in his letter to the Galatians that "it was because of a bodily ailment" (Galatians 4:13 esv) that he was able to preach the gospel to them at first. Lord, may my ailments and disability give me opportunity to share the gospel too. Help me to be bold and effective so that more people might know the good news and trust in You as Savior.

**JESUS**, I love reading about how You healed those with a disability! How huge crowds of people would bring to You those who were lame, unseeing, crippled, and mute. How they would lay these people before You and You would heal them—each and every one! How "the crowd was amazed! Those who hadn't been able to speak were talking, the crippled were made well, the lame were walking, and the blind could see again! And they praised the God of Israel" (Matthew 15:31 NLT). I believe You still have all the power to heal, and I know You will heal me fully, if not in this world, then in heaven forever when I am with You. So I praise You now! How great You are!

Show me the people who are just starting their journey of dealing with disability, Lord. Let me be a help and encouragement to them because I am farther down the road and have experiences and knowledge that can help them.

**LORD**, this scripture is such a breath of fresh air every time I read it. "They who wait for the Lord shall renew their strength; they shall mount up with wings like eagles; they shall run and not be weary; they shall walk and not faint" (Isaiah 40:31 esv). I wait for You, Lord, and I trust in this truth. I live in this promise!

# DISAPPOINTMENT

*Even though the fig trees have no blossoms, and
there are no grapes on the vines; even though the
olive crop fails, and the fields lie empty and barren;
even though the flocks die in the fields, and the cattle
barns are empty, yet I will rejoice in the LORD!
I will be joyful in the God of my salvation! The
Sovereign LORD is my strength! He makes me as
surefooted as a deer, able to tread upon the heights.*

HABAKKUK 3:17–19 NLT

Can we rejoice as Habakkuk did? Even if we struggle through disappointment after disappointment
after disappointment, will we, like he, rejoice in the
Lord anyway? No one can deny that life is full of
letdowns—big and small ones every single day. But
when our joy is based not on whether our earthly
hopes and expectations are met but rather on the
certainty that Jesus Christ is our salvation from sin
and our hope for eternity, then we will have strength
and stability even in the most uncertain times in
this world.

**LORD**, lately I feel like I just can't catch a break. It seems like my hopes keep getting dashed, all my plans keep getting ruined. Please show me what You want me to learn in these situations. Please help me not to get too discouraged. Show me Your perfect plans for my life.

**FATHER**, please show me and forgive me of my sin. I know some of the disappointments in my life come about because I'm seeking the wrong things. I pray that You would help me to seek first Your kingdom and Your righteousness before seeking anything else.

Are these disappointments part of Your discipline for me, Lord? If so, please help me to endure them well and learn from them. Even if I don't like it right now, even though it's painful and hard, I want to be able to appreciate Your discipline. Remind me that You are only doing what is best for me. I believe Your Word that says Your discipline is always good for me so that I might share in Your holiness and that I will reap a harvest of peace when I am trained by Your discipline (Hebrews 12:7–11).

Even though I am so disappointed by this situation right now, God, please help me not to grow weary in doing good (Galatians 6:9–10).

**FATHER,** help me to remember not to envy those who do wrong, not to want what they have but to respect and fear You, knowing You are where my future lies. Make it clear in my mind that I will be rewarded by following You. That in You my "hope will not be disappointed" (Proverbs 23:18 NLT). Help me not to compare myself to others and envy what they have that I don't. Help me to keep my eyes on You alone!

**LORD,** lead me to the places in Your Word where I can learn from Your people who dealt with disappointment. I think of Sarah who so wanted the child of Your promise yet must have been disappointed each month until she conceived Isaac. I think of Joseph being sold by his brothers into slavery—and Moses when he learned he would not enter in the Promised Land. Thank You for the lessons the heroes of the faith can teach me.

**LORD**, when I am deeply disappointed and discouraged, give me new encouragement through all kinds of sources, especially my loved ones. In turn, show me how to be a source of encouragement to my loved ones who may be going through their own deep disappointments.

Another setback has me feeling like totally giving up on this dream, God. But I know that with humans, some things are impossible, but with You "all things are possible" (Matthew 19:26 ESV). So I pray You will continue to guide me and lead me, to confirm that this dream is still Your will for me. Help me to discern if these disappointments are attacks from the enemy and You want me to stay the course or if You want me to change tack.

# DISHONESTY

*Thomas said to him, "Lord, we don't know where
you are going, so how can we know the way?" Jesus
answered, "I am the way and the truth and the life.
No one comes to the Father except through me."*

JOHN 14:5–6 NIV

Truth matters, and as Christians our whole way of life
is to follow Truth because we follow Jesus. He is the
Way, the *Truth*, and the Life. We know how much
truth matters because dishonesty creates distrust,
which breaks relationships and causes confusion
and chaos. Dishonesty destroys. When we find ourselves dealing with a stressful, dishonest situation,
our hope is in drawing closer to the one who has
promised, "There is nothing hidden that will not be
disclosed, and nothing concealed that will not be
known or brought out into the open" (Luke 8:17 NIV).

**FATHER**, someone I once trusted has lied to me in a big way, and now I don't know how to trust this person ever again. Should the relationship end or should we try to mend it? I know You want me to forgive, and I can do that with Your help, but I need wisdom to know whether or not to ever trust this person again. Please show me what to do and give me peace.

**JESUS**, please help me to be faithful and true in even the little things of life. Any compromising of honesty at all leads me further away from You. Forgive me for any little white lies and subtle, seemingly inconsequential untruths.

**LORD**, I messed up and told a big lie, and now I'm dealing with the consequences. I know I deserve them, for we reap what we sow. And I'm so sorry I sinned in this way. I thank You for extending to me Your grace and forgiveness, and I pray that those I lied to will do the same. In the meantime, show me what I can do to build back their trust.

"Teach me your way, O Lord, that I may walk in your truth; unite my heart to fear your name" (Psalm 86:11 esv).

**JESUS**, remind me regularly of the words You shared in Luke 16:10–11 (NLT): "If you are faithful in little things, you will be faithful in large ones. But if you are dishonest in little things, you won't be honest with greater responsibilities. And if you are untrustworthy about worldly wealth, who will trust you with the true riches of heaven?" Help me apply this wisdom and share it with others.

**LORD**, I don't want to have lying lips, which You hate. So I pray that You would help me to act faithfully and, in so doing, bring You delight (Proverbs 12:22).

**FATHER**, dishonesty in my workplace has me tearing my hair out! It has created such a stressful atmosphere these days. Please reveal the truth quickly and help our team get back to being a productive and positive work environment.

**FATHER**, "lead me in your truth and teach me, for you are the God of my salvation; for you I wait all the day long" (Psalm 25:5 ESV).

# ELDERLY PARENTS

*"Honor your father and mother" (this is the first*
*commandment with a promise), "that it may go well*
*with you and that you may live long in the land."*
Ephesians 6:2–3 esv

That children are to honor their parents is a lifelong command—and a promised blessing. When adult children are faced with the uncertainties that come with elderly parents and their care, God would have us remember that He is good and He is with us, wanting to reward us for obeying His command to honor our moms and dads. Yet with age comes loss of capabilities and mental capacities, and too often the elderly are considered among "the least of these." But Jesus tells His followers that "whatever you did for one of the least of these brothers and sisters of mine, you did for me" (Matthew 25:40 niv). We can respect and honor and care for elderly parents thinking about how we are serving Jesus Himself. And remembering that someday we in turn will be elderly parents looking to our own children to take their part in caring for us.

**HEAVENLY FATHER**, thank You for my earthly parents. They gave me life and care, and now it's my turn to take good care of them as they age and decline. Show me how to do that in the best ways possible. Give my parents and myself grace and patience with each other. Fill us with Your love and peace.

**LORD,** Your Word says to "listen to your father who gave you life, and do not despise your mother when she is old" (Proverbs 23:22 ESV). The command is clear to respect my parents no matter their age. Thank You for this opportunity to love and honor them near the end of their earthly lives.

These experiences caring for my elderly parents will humble us all, Jesus. So please remind us what a good thing that is. Because when we are humble, we are more like You! (Philippians 2:5–11)

**GOD**, we believe that You oppose "the proud" and give "grace to the humble" (James 4:6 NLT). Today I ask for You to pour out upon me that grace as I honor and serve my parents in these uncertain times.

**LORD**, this is such a hard season of life as I juggle my busy schedule and the needs of my elderly parents. Give me the strength and stamina I need! Give me wisdom and help me to manage my time well.

**JESUS**, I want to serve my parents like You served others so well in Your earthly ministry. Keep me hungry for Your Word. Strengthen and encourage me with the many examples in the Gospels of how You served and healed and cared for people. Continually bring to my mind this scripture: "Jesus did many other things as well. If every one of them were written down, I suppose that even the whole world would not have room for the books that would be written" (John 21:25 NIV).

**FATHER**, this time I still have with my elderly parents is meaningful. Help me to value it as the gift that it is. Help me to remember that even in the struggles, my parents have wisdom and love to give me, while I get to show them my deep love and appreciation in return.

# ENEMIES

*Pray, too, that we will be rescued from wicked
and evil people, for not everyone is a believer.
But the Lord is faithful; he will strengthen
you and guard you from the evil one.*

2 Thessalonians 3:2–3 nlt

---

Our worst enemy Satan is always prowling around, looking to destroy us. And we are under attack in all sorts of ways from all sorts of wicked people in this sinful world. But God is always faithful. He strengthens and guards us. His Word promises: "The Lord will keep you from all evil; he will keep your life. The Lord will keep your going out and your coming in from this time forth and forevermore" (Psalm 121:7–8 esv). So keep your focus on Him, knowing that because you believe, because you trust in God, because you have made Him your refuge, "he will command his angels. . .to guard you in all your ways" (Psalm 91:11 esv).

I believe my best weapon against enemies is prayer—and not just prayer for protection *from* them but sincere prayer *for* them. Please change their hearts, Lord! Let them be full of love and mercy instead of cruelty and evil.

**ALMIGHTY GOD**, help me to continually remember that "though I walk in the midst of trouble, you preserve my life; you stretch out your hand against the wrath of my enemies, and your right hand delivers me" (Psalm 138:7 ESV).

**LORD**, when my enemies attack me, please give me self-control and wisdom. Remind me that I am to "not take revenge...but leave room for God's wrath, for it is written: 'It is mine to avenge; I will repay,' says the Lord" (Romans 12:19 NIV).

**LORD**, it is so hard to follow Your Word when it says I should bless those who persecute me, that I should not curse them but pray that You will bless them (Romans 12:14). Yet because I want to please You, because I want to obey You in this, no matter how difficult it is to do so, I pray that You would help me to have a heart and love for people like You do.

**FATHER**, please work a miracle in this situation like only You can. It all seems so bizarre, so unfair that this person is treating me this way. So I pray You would turn this enemy of mine into my friend. And I have faith that You can do so because nothing is impossible for You!

**LORD**, Your Word promises that if my way pleases You, then You will make even my enemies be at peace with me (Proverbs 16:7). I need that peace, Lord. I need it now. So I pray You would show me what of my own ways I must change so that I will please You. Then give me the strength to work on that change while I focus on You and Your promised peace.

**LORD**, at one time I was Your enemy when I was still lost in my sin. Thank You for not rejecting me but offering me endless love and grace! Help me to extend that same love and grace to my enemies.

**GOD,** Your Word says I should do things like feed my enemies and give them water when they are hungry and thirsty, not take revenge. Help me to leave revenge to Your righteous anger. Give me the strength and courage to not be overcome by evil but rather to overcome evil by doing good (Romans 12:21).

# FAMILY DYNAMICS

*But those who won't care for their relatives, especially those in their own household, have denied the true faith. Such people are worse than unbelievers.*
1 Timothy 5:8 nlt

---

This scripture makes it clear—our families are important. We should care for and look after one another as best we can. At the same time, our families are often the source of a lot of conflict and strife. Although we know each other's flaws, see each other's worst side, and often stress each other out, we still love each other dearly. We are deeply connected to each other, by household, by biology, and/or by adoption. To help us navigate the issues and uncertainties that arise in dealing with family dynamics, we can answer the call to real love found in 1 Corinthians 13: "Love is patient and kind. Love is not jealous or boastful or proud or rude. It does not demand its own way. It is not irritable, and it keeps no record of being wronged. It does not rejoice about injustice but rejoices whenever the truth wins out. Love never gives up, never loses faith, is always hopeful, and endures through every circumstance" (13:4–7 nlt).

With so much fighting and strife in the world, Lord, it seems awful that it happens even in our homes and within our families. Please bring us peace. Help us to realize we can have good, healthy conflict and communication without fighting and hurting one another.

**JESUS**, fill us with gratitude for the ways You bless us. Although we don't deserve Your grace and mercy, You still pour it upon us so freely. So I pray You would help us to give each other grace and mercy as generously as You give it to us.

Your Word is full of stories of families who had plenty of problems and dysfunction going on, Lord. They were broken and flawed, just like me and my family. Yet You still used them to accomplish Your perfect plans. I know You can use my family too, Lord. So I pray You would heal our brokenness and forgive our flaws. That You would use me and my family to further Your kingdom.

**FATHER**, please give me wisdom to use good boundaries with my family. Just because I love them dearly does not mean I can disrespect their space, time, and responsibilities, nor they mine. So I pray, Lord, that You would help us see the value of boundaries and how they help us keep peace and good relationship.

**JESUS**, please wipe away my tears and bring me comfort from the pain of a family relationship that is broken, seemingly beyond repair. I never thought things would turn out like this, and my heart aches every day. I pray for the person who has broken off. Most of all, I pray that not only would she seek You first but that she would let You soften her heart.

**GOD**, remind my family that we love because You first loved us (1 John 4:19). And that You Yourself are love (1 John 4:8, 16).

When my family feels pulled and stretched in every direction, God, help us find ways to unclutter our lives and schedules so that we have more margin and more peace, more time to work through conflict, to calm waves, to just laugh and relax.

**GOD**, it is good when my family dwells together in unity (Psalm 133:1). Please help us do so!

**FATHER**, show us the bad habits in our family that we need to get rid of. Show us the things we do that hurt our health, hinder our communication, and give us lots of stress. Help us to banish these bad habits from our lives.

**LORD**, please help me and my family to work with each other and not against each other. Help us to be like a great team whose members help, encourage, and support each other.

**LORD,** help me and my family's love for each other to be genuine. Help us to abhor what is evil and hold fast to what is good (Romans 12:9).

Busy schedules can take such a toll on my family, God. Help us to be intentional about spending quality time together, not just quick moments here and there. Those are nice, but we also need unhurried time to just enjoy each other's company. Help us to crave the fun times and good fellowship together.

# FEARS FOR THE FUTURE

*Listen, you who say, "Today or tomorrow we will go to this or that city, spend a year there, carry on business and make money." Why, you do not even know what will happen tomorrow. What is your life? You are a mist that appears for a little while and then vanishes. Instead, you ought to say, "If it is the Lord's will, we will live and do this or that." As it is, you boast in your arrogant schemes. All such boasting is evil. If anyone, then, knows the good they ought to do and doesn't do it, it is sin for them.*

JAMES 4:13–17 NIV

The hard truth is that none of us know anything for certain about what will happen in the future. Our life, our every breath come from God (Acts 17:25), and our times are in His hands (Psalm 31:15). And when we humbly accept the reality that nothing in the future is guaranteed no matter how we plan for, hope for, and expect it, we can choose to rest in God's sovereignty and hold our plans and expectations very loosely. We can speak this truth to ourselves and to others daily: "If it is the Lord's will, we will live and do this or that."

"I am trusting you, O Lord, saying, 'You are my God!'
My future is in your hands" (Psalm 31:14–15 NLT).

It's overwhelming to think of what tomorrow could
hold in this crazy world, God! Things seem more
uncertain by the day. Help me not to fret about the
future though. Nothing—"neither death nor life,
neither angels nor demons, neither our fears for
today nor our worries about tomorrow—not even
the powers of hell" (Romans 8:38 NLT)—can separate me from Your love, and that's all I really
need to know.

**LORD**, You said to Your people, "I know the plans I have for you. . . . They are plans for good and not for disaster, to give you a future and a hope" (Jeremiah 29:11 NLT). And so I trust that You have good plans for me, ones that will give me a future and a hope. Hallelujah!

**CREATOR GOD**, I believe I am Your masterpiece. I believe You created me anew in Christ Jesus so that I can do the good things You planned for me long ago (Ephesians 2:10). Since I know I am Your masterpiece, help me to live like it—with gratitude and confidence and joy!

No matter what my future holds, Lord, I believe You will instruct me and teach me in the way I should go. You will counsel me with Your eye upon me (Psalm 32:8).

**FATHER**, I can surely see how "the world is passing away along with its desires" but I believe with all my heart that "whoever does the will of God abides forever" (1 John 2:17 ESV). Continue to reveal to me, Lord, what Your will is for my life.

**LORD**, I believe You will work out Your plans for my life, for Your never-ending faithful love endures forever (Psalm 138:8).

Undeniably, my future holds death, Lord, because no one lives forever here on earth. Although I have no idea when my earthly death will be—for You alone know the number of my days—I am so incredibly grateful that my eternal future is in heaven with You! I praise You because in Your great mercy, You have given me new birth into a living hope through the resurrection of Jesus Christ from the dead, and into an inheritance that can never perish, spoil, or fade. Thank You for keeping this inheritance in heaven for me, and for the fact that through faith I am shielded by Your power until I receive the salvation that's ready to be revealed on the last day (1 Peter 1:3–5).

**GOD**, I greatly rejoice in this day, this moment, even though now for a little while I may have to suffer grief in all kinds of trials. I know troubles have come so the genuineness of my faith—which is of greater worth than gold, which perishes even though refined by fire—may be proven and result in praise, glory, and honor when Jesus Christ is revealed. Though I have not seen Him face-to-face, I do love Him with all my heart and soul. And even though I do not see Him now, I do believe in Him and am filled with a glorious joy that cannot be expressed in words. I find contentment and hope in the truth that because I trust Him, I will be rewarded with the saving of my soul (1 Peter 1:6–9).

# FEELING OUT
# OF CONTROL

*The heart of man plans his way,*
*but the LORD establishes his steps.*
PROVERBS 16:9 ESV

---

We like to make our plans and establish goals for
our lives. But if we hold to them too tightly, we
can be utterly overwhelmed and upended when
surprising events and circumstances veer us off
course. That out-of-control, uncertain feeling can
produce all sorts of anxiety. Thus, we must look
to the Lord constantly, knowing He lets us plan
our ways with the gifts, creativity, and free will
He has given us (and often approves and blesses
those plans we make when we seek to honor Him).
Yet He, the Lord of our lives, ultimately has all
sovereignty and control. He holds the map and
knows the course, and He determines the steps we
should take that are far better than any we could
ever dream up on our own.

**FATHER**, forgive me for how desperately I want control at times. I know that every blessing I have is from You. In fact, every breath I take is from You. I also know You are sovereign and in control. So I thank You for letting me have so much freedom to make my plans and do things I decide on, but I ask You to help me to always want to walk within Your will. Help me to hold loosely to my plans so that You can alter them any way You see fit. I trust You completely.

**LORD**, "Your word is a lamp to guide my feet and a light for my path" (Psalm 119:105 NLT). Show me Your will and way as I spend time in Your Word every day. Thank You for providing Your believers this guidebook for life.

Life feels chaotic right now, Father. Help me to trust in You with all my heart and lean not on my own understanding. Remind me to acknowledge You in everything I do! For I believe You direct my paths in the ways that are best for me (Proverbs 3:5–6).

**LORD**, You are in complete control—and You are greater, bigger, mightier than my anxious thoughts and worries. Teach me that my energy could be better spent in prayer than in the land of what-ifs. When I feel out of control, help me to see what I can control— which is choosing to spend more time in prayer because I can do that anytime, anywhere. Thank You for Your presence with me, hearing everything I say, and understanding what I cannot put into words. Please help me to listen well to Your answers and rest in Your resulting peace.

**LORD MOST HIGH**, I live in Your shelter and find rest in Your shadow. You alone are my refuge and place of safety. You will rescue me from every trap and protect me from every disease. You will cover me with Your feathers and shelter me with Your wings. Your faithful promises are my armor and protection. I don't need to be afraid of anything, night or day. I love You, Lord, and I trust in Your name. For I know that when I call on You, You will answer. You will rescue and honor me and reward me with salvation (Psalm 91).

**FATHER**, please give me unwavering confidence that You are for me and with me. Remind me that there is nothing coming my way that You can't overcome. No power is greater than You. Trusting You, I can rest in You today and every day, knowing that while I might not have everything under control, You absolutely do.

**FATHER**, sometimes when I'm feeling out of control, it's because I don't want to let go and accept that You may have other ideas. I want to make things happen the way I want them to happen. As a result, I end up trying to push open doors that You might intend to stay closed. Please forgive me. I ask for Your will to be done in Your good way and in Your good time.

# FINANCIAL STRESS

*"Look at the birds of the air: they neither sow nor reap nor gather into barns, and yet your heavenly Father feeds them. Are you not of more value than they? And which of you by being anxious can add a single hour to his span of life? And why are you anxious about clothing? Consider the lilies of the field, how they grow: they neither toil nor spin, yet I tell you, even Solomon in all his glory was not arrayed like one of these. But if God so clothes the grass of the field, which today is alive and tomorrow is thrown into the oven, will he not much more clothe you, O you of little faith? Therefore do not be anxious, saying, 'What shall we eat?' or 'What shall we drink?' or 'What shall we wear?' For the Gentiles seek after all these things, and your heavenly Father knows that you need them all. But seek first the kingdom of God and his righteousness, and all these things will be added to you."*

MATTHEW 6:26–33 ESV

---

The above is everything we need to know to deal with financial stress, yet still we fret at times. May we daily ask God sincerely to help us seek His kingdom and His righteousness first—for then we will experience how everything we truly need flows from Him.

**FATHER**, please forgive me for worrying about money. Help me to trust more in Your promises. In all that I do, help me to work with my whole heart, as working for You and not for men (Colossians 3:23). I want my work and my finances to honor You!

**LORD**, You are the one who created me and enabled me to work and earn money. And so I want to give back to You by giving to churches and ministries that share the good news, teach Your Word, and serve and care for others in Your name. Help me never to stress over being generous in this way. For giving back to You who gave to me in the first place is the best thing I can do with my money.

**GOD**, I want to honor You with my wealth and with the firstfruits of whatever I produce. Then You will bless me above and beyond what I need or desire (Proverbs 3:9–10).

**JESUS**, don't ever let me forget these words You said while preaching to the crowds on the mount: "No one can serve two masters, for either he will hate the one and love the other, or he will be devoted to the one and despise the other. You cannot serve God and money" (Matthew 6:24 ESV). May I every day serve You, my almighty God, not the almighty dollar.

**FATHER**, help me to remember that "wealth gained hastily will dwindle, but whoever gathers little by little will increase it" (Proverbs 13:11 ESV).

Even when finances are strained, help me to never stop being generous, Lord. For You have said, "Bring all the tithes into the storehouse so there will be enough food in my Temple. If you do. . .I will open the windows of heaven for you. I will pour out a blessing so great you won't have enough room to take it in! Try it! Put me to the test! Your crops will be abundant, for I will guard them from insects and disease. Your grapes will not fall from the vine before they are ripe. . . . Then all nations will call you blessed, for your land will be such a delight" (Malachi 3:10–12 NLT).

**FATHER**, when I feel worried about money, help me never to cheat in any way to try to get more. Help me to remember that "a good name is to be chosen rather than great riches, and favor is better than silver or gold" (Proverbs 22:1 ESV).

**LORD**, help me not to be stingy, for Your Word says, "A stingy man hastens after wealth and does not know that poverty will come upon him" (Proverbs 28:22 ESV).

**LORD**, help me never to take advantage of others, for Your Word says, "One who oppresses the poor to increase his wealth and one who gives gifts to the rich—both come to poverty" (Proverbs 22:16 NIV).

**GOD**, I don't want to trust in money, which is so unreliable. I want my trust to be in You alone, the one who richly gives me all I need for my enjoyment. I want to use my money to do good. I want to be rich in good works and generous to those in need, always ready to share with others. I believe that by doing these things, I am storing up treasure as a good foundation for the future so that I may experience true life (1 Timothy 6:17–19).

# FORECLOSURE

*My God will supply every need of yours*
*according to his riches in glory in Christ Jesus.*
PHILIPPIANS 4:19 ESV

---

Financial tragedy like a foreclosure surely makes for uncertain times. So many stressful factors can contribute to reaching such a low point—a point from which we can feel it's totally impossible to rise again. But God is faithful and will carry us through any difficulty as we seek to honor and obey Him. We must remember that there is no pit, not even the deepest money pit, that He cannot rescue us from. His resources to help us are endless, for "the earth is the LORD's, and everything in it. The world and all its people belong to him. For he laid the earth's foundation on the seas and built it on the ocean depths" (Psalm 24:1–2 NLT). It is in that truth our hope must rest.

**FATHER**, this foreclosure feels much too much to bear. My family and I feel overwhelmed and humiliated. It has definitely humbled us. Remind us that humility is a good thing, that You are to be glorified in all things, not us. We pray that You would come to our rescue and let others see Your power and Your provision as You lift us out of this mess we're in. Please make Your good result from our situation. All honor and glory be to You, the one who is with us in good times and bad, in plenty and in want.

**JESUS**, even with a foreclosure looming, help me to be like the poor widow who put two small copper coins—all she had to live on—in the offering box. I want to be generous and show that I trust You to provide for me. I can give everything I have to You, and I will still always have what I need.

It's so confusing, Father, to go through all this legal and financial paperwork. I just want to sit and cry, I'm so overwhelmed. Please give me peace, and encourage me with extraordinary kindness during this difficult time.

**GOD**, the economy and loans and mortgages and interest rates, all those things are so complicated. As we face foreclosure, remind us that we are not alone in this mess. Many others have made the same mistakes. We cannot undo what is already done, so help us to focus instead on the future. Help us to learn from the past and move forward. Please give us the wisdom to plan and manage our finances more carefully this time.

We are grieving the loss of our house, Lord. Help us not to tamp down our emotions. At the same time, keep us from falling into total despair. Help us to grieve well and wisely so that we can move forward with peace and hope.

**JESUS,** we are so sad to lose this house to foreclosure. Yet we pray You would help us to remember our forever home is with You. Help us keep in mind Your words: "Don't store up treasures here on earth, where moths eat them and rust destroys them, and where thieves break in and steal. Store your treasures in heaven, where moths and rust cannot destroy, and thieves do not break in and steal. Wherever your treasure is, there the desires of your heart will also be" (Matthew 6:19–21 NLT).

# GOVERNMENT, ECONOMY, AND POLITICS

*Blessed is the nation whose God is the LORD,*
*the people whom he has chosen as his heritage!*

PSALM 33:12 ESV

The state of government, the economy, and politics feels grimmer and darker by the day. But God sits on His throne above it all, with a perspective far higher and better than ours. We cannot possibly see and know all the ways He is working out His plans and purposes, but we trust He is sovereign and good. Rather than suffer from worry and fear, we can focus on God's Word and prayer to draw closer to the one who changes times and seasons, removes and sets up kings, and gives wisdom to the wise and knowledge to those who have understanding (Daniel 2:21).

Kingship belongs to You, Lord! You rule over the nations (Psalm 22:28)!

**GOD**, even when I disagree at times with what's going on in our government, economy, and politics, I pray You would help me to be a law-abiding citizen who is "subject to the governing authorities." I believe Your Word that says, "For there is no authority except from God, and those that exist have been instituted by God" (Romans 13:1 ESV).

**HEAVENLY FATHER**, remind me "to be submissive to rulers and authorities, to be obedient, [and most of all] to be ready for every good work" (Titus 3:1 ESV).

**LORD**, thank You for the freedom of religion and freedom of speech in our nation. I pray we always have those! I'm grateful that because of those freedoms, we Christians can practice our faith in You and openly share it with others. I pray for those Christians who are in nations where they are persecuted for their faith. Protect and sustain them, Lord! Let many more come to faith in You because of their great courage and ministry!

**LORD**, I am subject for Your sake to every human institution, whether it be to the emperor as supreme, or to governors as sent by You to punish those who do evil and to praise those who do good. I believe Your Word that says this is for Your will, that by doing good I should put to silence the ignorance of foolish people. Help me to live as one who is free, because I am, but help me not to use my freedom as a cover-up for evil. I live as Your servant. I want to obey Your Word that says, "Honor everyone. Love the brotherhood. Fear God. Honor the emperor" (1 Peter 2:17 ESV).

**GOD**, Your Word urges me to pray for all people. So I come to You today, asking You to help them. I intercede on their behalf and give thanks to You for them. I pray this way for kings and all who are in authority so that we can live peaceful and quiet lives marked by godliness and dignity. I believe this is good and pleases You because You want everyone to be saved and to understand the truth (1 Timothy 2:1–3 NLT).

I'm so very grateful that no matter what happens in this world, my true citizenship is in heaven, and from there I wait for You to come, Jesus my Savior (Philippians 3:20)!

**LORD**, when I feel anxious about the affairs of the world, give me peace. Help me to remember the truth that while government leaders may have many plans (either for good or for evil), it is Your purpose that prevails over them all (Proverbs 19:21 NLT).

Help me and all Your people to remember what You said, Lord—that "if my people, who are called by my name, will humble themselves and pray and seek my face and turn from their wicked ways, then I will hear from heaven, and I will forgive their sin and heal their land" (2 Chronicles 7:14 NIV).

You fill me with peace and I praise You, Jesus, for You are "far above all rule and authority, power and dominion, and every name that is invoked, not only in the present age but also in the one to come" (Ephesians 1:21 NIV).

**JESUS**, in the midst of all the chaos going on in the world, I trust that the gospel is being preached in the whole world, a testimony to all nations so that everyone has the opportunity to trust in You as Savior (Matthew 24:14). Continue to show me my part in that wonderful work!

# GRIEVING

*The Lord is near to the brokenhearted
and saves the crushed in spirit.*

PSALM 34:18 ESV

---

Grieving is hard but important. It's not just about the loss of a loved one—though that is the worst type of grief. But giving ourselves time, space, and grace to grieve any type of loss—of a loved one, of a relationship that is broken, of a job, of a home, of a church and community because of a move, or whatever it might be—is essential to be able to heal and move forward in a healthy and ready-for-what's-next kind of way. Squelching our feelings doesn't make them go away. Suppressed negative emotions can cause all sorts of mental and physical health problems. And God knows our feelings anyway (Psalm 139) whether or not we admit them to ourselves or others, so there's no need to hide them from Him. Through prayer and lament, we can bring our wounds before Him, asking Him to bind them up as His Word promises He will (Psalm 147:3).

**LORD,** I thank You that I do "not grieve as others do who have no hope" (1 Thessalonians 4:13 ESV). Let Your steadfast love be upon me as I put all my hope in You (Psalm 33:22)!

Some days I just feel numb over this loss, God, but that's scaring me. It doesn't seem healthy. I know I have all kinds of emotions to deal with, but they seem bottled up tight right now. Please help me release them and deal with them. Then give me Your unsurpassed peace, Your calm amid the storm.

**FATHER,** help me to deal with all these deep feelings of grief in ways that are good for me. Guard me from turning to alcohol or drugs, or eating too much, or anything unhealthy to try to cope. Please control me when I feel like I don't have any self-control because my emotions are all over the place. Help me give myself and my grief up to You.

**LORD,** help me find and create good habits in a healthy exercise that I enjoy, knowing doing so will aid me in releasing some of my emotions. My sweat and tears can mingle together, which sounds very much like something I need in this moment.

**FATHER**, You are merciful, and You are the source of all comfort. I believe that You comfort me in all my troubles so that I can then comfort others. You are preparing me today so that at some point tomorrow, when others are troubled, I will be able to give them the same comfort You have given me (2 Corinthians 1:3–4 NLT).

**LORD**, my spirit feels as if it is crushed into infinite pieces. Will I ever feel whole and put together again? Thankfully, You have promised that these are the times You are near, the times when You will save those who, like me, are broken (Psalm 34:18).

Will I always have this horrible hollow feeling of grief, God? Please fill up the empty places with Your love. Shower me with Your light and hope.

**FATHER**, my vision feels blurred from grief (Psalm 6:7). I feel as if I can't view anything with a good and right perspective right now because it's so hard to focus on anything other than my sorrow. Be my vision for me, please. Help me to see what You would have me see with clarity and discernment.

**ALMIGHTY GOD**, my flesh and my heart may fail, but You are the strength of my heart and my portion forever (Psalm 73:26).

**LORD**, "remember your promise to me; it is my only hope. Your promise revives me; it comforts me in all my troubles" (Psalm 119:49–50 NLT).

"The Lord is my Shepherd. I will have everything I need. He lets me rest in fields of green grass. He leads me beside the quiet waters. He makes me strong again. He leads me in the way of living right with Himself which brings honor to His name. Yes, even if I walk through the valley of the shadow of death, I will not be afraid of anything, because You are with me. You have a walking stick with which to guide and one with which to help. These comfort me. You are making a table of food ready for me in front of those who hate me. You have poured oil on my head. I have everything I need. For sure, You will give me goodness and loving-kindness all the days of my life. Then I will live with You in Your house forever" (Psalm 23 NLV).

# HEALTH SCARES (WAITING FOR MEDICAL TEST RESULTS)

*Dear friend, I pray that you may enjoy good
health and that all may go well with you,
even as your soul is getting along well.*

3 JOHN 1:2 NIV

---

Just as John prayed for his friend in this passage, we pray for ourselves and our loved ones to enjoy good health. But unfortunately, we know that illness, injury, and disease afflict us all from time to time. Although some diagnoses are scarier and more uncertain than others, no matter what our circumstances, we are encouraged to "not lose heart. Though outwardly we are wasting away, yet inwardly we are being renewed day by day. For our light and momentary troubles are achieving for us an eternal glory that far outweighs them all. So we fix our eyes not on what is seen, but on what is unseen, since what is seen is temporary, but what is unseen is eternal" (2 Corinthians 4:16–18 NIV).

**LORD,** I am afraid. These symptoms could mean a myriad of terrible diagnoses. Please let these test results come back negative. Please give me a clean bill of health.

**FATHER,** as I wait and have tests done, I realize that anxiety won't help anything. In fact, it could even make my blood pressure seem to be at a dangerous level even if it's truly not. So I pray that You would please give me supernatural peace right now. Don't let anxiety contribute to any false test results.

I don't know what to do if the diagnosis I fear is what becomes my reality, God. What will happen to me and my loved ones? I feel like I am about to panic. Please calm me down, Lord. Remind me of Your love and care and that You are with me every moment.

**FATHER**, please let me feel Your love in tangible ways as I endure these medical tests and wait on their results. Thank You for my family and friends who are helping me. Thank You for warm blankets and a comforting touch from health professionals. Help me to notice and focus on these little blessings and comforts.

It seems impossible that this test result could come back negative, but nothing is impossible for You, Almighty God! I pray that You would show us a miracle like only You can!

**FATHER**, I know that some of my bad habits have led to this health scare. I have forgotten and ignored Your truth that my body is a temple of the Holy Spirit within me. I have not glorified You with my body (1 Corinthians 6:19–20). Please forgive me. Whatever the outcome of this health scare, show me how to do better from now on at honoring You with the body with which You have blessed me.

"Heal me, O Lord, and I shall be healed; save me, and I shall be saved, for you are my praise" (Jeremiah 17:14 ESV).

**FATHER**, I believe all my days are known and numbered by You. No matter what the result of this test, no matter what my diagnosis, I know You won't be surprised and that You will work all things together for good (Romans 8:28). I love You, and I'm so grateful to be Your child.

**JESUS**, You bore our sins in Your body on the cross, that we might die to sin and live to righteousness. By Your wounds I have been healed (1 Peter 2:24). Nothing can take that healing and hope away from me. And for that I am so grateful!

# HOUSE HUNTING

*"From one man he made all the nations, that they should inhabit the whole earth; and he marked out their appointed times in history and the boundaries of their lands. God did this so that they would seek him and perhaps reach out for him and find him, though he is not far from any one of us. 'For in him we live and move and have our being.' As some of your own poets have said, 'We are his offspring.'"*

ACTS 17:26–28 NIV

---

All the work that goes into moving is stressful enough. Add in the state of the economy and the housing market, and finding the right home can turn into a nightmare. Just when we think we've found the perfect place, we discover it's already under contract, the price is too high, or the street traffic is too much. Then once we finally find the house that seems to be working out, there's all the little details: offers, counteroffers, inspections, etc.! God knows, cares, and desires we seek Him in the process. We can let Him carry the load of house-hunting stress, knowing He has promised to provide for all our needs and will surely help us find a good place to live.

In the midst of the stress of house hunting, Lord, help me not to forget how blessed I am. You have provided for me in the past and will continue to do so. Fill me with joy and great expectation for how You will show Your love and care through this house-hunting process.

Give us wisdom and discernment as we look at homes, Lord. Help us to see the issues that might make purchase an unwise choice.

"Location, location, location," they say. Yet it's not what I want but what You want, God. What do You say is the best location for me and my family for this season of life?

I am weary, Lord. House hunting is not going like I'd hoped and planned. Please give me renewed strength and energy. Help me keep an upbeat attitude. Remind me that You are with me through this process.

**FATHER**, please let the seller accept our offer! It's fair and fits our budget. And we feel peaceful about it. Help us not to unwisely get into a bidding war. If this house is the one for us, please let this deal go through. If not, help us to be content with that—that You closed the door and will show us something better for our family.

**JESUS**, I'm so thankful that no matter what house I live in here on earth, You are preparing a perfect place for me to live forever in heaven. You have said, "Let not your hearts be troubled. Believe in God; believe also in me. In my Father's house are many rooms. If it were not so, would I have told you that I go to prepare a place for you? And if I go and prepare a place for you, I will come again and will take you to myself, that where I am you may be also" (John 14:1–3 ESV).

# INFERTILITY AND MISCARRIAGE

*Your eyes saw my unformed substance; in your book
were written, every one of them, the days that were
formed for me, when as yet there was none of them.*
PSALM 139:16 ESV

There is so much excitement and hopefulness in the
dreams of pregnancy and babies. But when those
dreams are shattered by infertility and miscarriage,
it's agonizing devastation. It's often a lonely time
too, when we feel like no one else understands. Yet
infertility and miscarriage are a common struggle
for many couples, and when we reach out to connect
with others who have had similar experiences, we find
support and comfort. And most of all we can reach out
to our heavenly Father who knows our hearts better
than anyone else. He knows how much we long to
nurture new life in our wombs and bring a new child
into the world. So we must cling to Him no matter
the outcome, knowing that He both gives and takes
away and we can still choose to say, "Blessed be His
name" (Job 1:21)!

**LORD**, we have been hoping to get pregnant, but our hopes are dashed month after month. I feel like the psalmist who wrote, "How long will you forget me? Forever? How long will you look the other way? How long must I struggle with anguish in my soul, with sorrow in my heart every day?" (Psalm 13:1–2 NLT). So I pray that You will speak to my spirit, comfort my heart, apply a balm to my soul.

Hannah was in deep anguish like I am, God. She desperately wanted a son. Thank You for her story in the Bible. Please bless me with a child, just as You blessed her with Samuel (1 Samuel 1).

**GOD**, Sarah was in total disbelief when You said she would have a child at her age (Genesis 18). It does seem impossible for me to have a child after all this time of waiting and trying with no baby conceived. But Your good Word reminds me that nothing is ever impossible for You, that You can choose to bring new life into the world at any time through me. I pray that You would allow me that blessing.

**LORD**, Your Word says: "By faith Sarah herself received power to conceive, even when she was past the age, since she considered him faithful who had promised" (Hebrews 11:11 ESV). I too consider You faithful! I pray that, as You did with Sarah, You, my Creator, would give me power to conceive against all odds!

**LORD,** I ache over the loss of this baby who died in my womb, one who had already stolen my heart. I struggle with wondering if something I did caused his or her death. Did I exercise too much and not rest enough? Did I not take enough prenatal vitamins? Please help me to stop beating myself up. Protect me from guilt-ridden lies from the enemy. I trust that You saw this precious little one forming in my womb, and You knew exactly the number of his or her days. My baby is now with You, perfectly loved and cared for forever. Please comfort my sorrow as I rest in that truth.

**LORD,** I'm desperate to get pregnant again, yet also so scared I will lose the baby again. Please give me peace and comfort. Help me to trust in Your goodness and sovereignty even when I feel confused, afraid, and sad.

**FATHER**, help my husband with his pain and frustration with infertility. We experience all our emotions differently. I pray You would help him connect with other men who are believers and have experienced infertility, men who can support and encourage him.

**GOD**, Your Word says that Isaac prayed to You for his wife, because she was barren. And You granted his prayer, making a way for his wife Rebekah to conceive (Genesis 25). I know my husband is praying for me too, just like Isaac did. Please answer our prayers and help us conceive!

**LORD**, surround me with comfort and wisdom from women who know firsthand about the frustration and pain of infertility or miscarriage. I feel so lonely sometimes. When I see other women who are pregnant, while I am not, and have children, which I do not, sorrow overtakes me. I need empathy and encouragement from women who understand and care. I pray You would provide me with that.

**FATHER**, I cannot deny this anger and jealousy I feel toward women who seem to get pregnant so easily and then are blessed with births, and I am not. I confess my anger and envy to You. Please help me channel this emotion, this energy, in a better way, one that will help rather than hinder me.

**LORD**, I love You most of all. If conceiving a child is not Your will for me, please help me to accept that peacefully. Help me to grieve over this new reality in healthy ways and then move forward. Open to me an outlet where I can use my love of children to further Your kingdom, to spread Your light and love.

**LORD**, is adoption or foster care Your plan for our family? If so, I would pray that You would fill us with joy and excitement over those opportunities and guide us in them. You are our one true God and Savior, and we praise You and worship You!

# INSOMNIA

*By the seventh day God had finished the work he
had been doing; so on the seventh day he rested
from all his work. Then God blessed the seventh
day and made it holy, because on it he rested from
all the work of creating that he had done.*

GENESIS 2:2–3 NIV

---

Sleep is so important for our health and well-being,
and when we can't seem to get it, life can be absolutely
miserable. Our physical health, our mental health,
our relationships, our work—everything suffers if
we're struggling with insomnia. At times we might
need to seek professional advice from a doctor and/
or psychologist. And we can *always* consult with our
Creator, the one who rested and intends for us to rest
too, and His Son, our perfect Savior, Jesus, who gave
us an example of when and how to rest.

**GOD**, there is a specific situation that's causing me so much stress and it's drastically affecting my sleep. You know what is happening in my life. You know how much I stew and fret over it. So I pray that You would work in this situation and bring Your resolution to it, that You would provide Your calm amid my chaos.

**FATHER**, it seems like every night my body is tired, but my mind just won't shut down to let me fall into a deep sleep. Please help! I feel like I'm in a never-ending cycle of exhaustion and anxiety.

**LORD**, help me to choose good nutrition and exercise for my body. Help me to stop bad eating habits and reduce my computer, phone, and TV time late at night. Please bring to my mind all the practical things I can do to encourage good sleep and reveal the ways that I can drop the habits that hinder it. Remind me not to try to make too many changes at once but to begin slowly as I find my way to rest in You.

I'm focusing on these words tonight, Lord: "In peace I will lie down and sleep, for you alone, O LORD, will keep me safe" (Psalm 4:8 NLT).

Tonight, God, help me to accept it calmly if I can't seem to fully rest my mind. For I realize that panicking about it will hinder rather than help me. Help me to at least rest and relax my body. If my mind wants to stay busy, please bring to mind all those who are in need of prayer including myself, my loved ones, and the world. If it be Your will, may this also be a time when I rehearse Bible verses in my mind, praying the scriptures right back to You, giving You delight and myself comfort.

**LORD**, please guide the doctors and mental health professionals who are trying to help me get more sleep.

**FATHER**, Your Word says You give sleep to Your beloved (Psalm 127:2). I am Your beloved, so please let it be so. Please give me sleep tonight! And if sleep doesn't come, tell me what You would have me know, think on, pray about.

**FATHER**, please show me the root causes of the anxiety that's keeping me awake at night. If it's a sin I am entertaining, please help me to recognize and confess it. If it's hurt or anger I am holding on to, please show me how it can be resolved.

**JESUS**, You said, "Come to me, all who labor and are heavy laden, and I will give you rest" (Matthew 11:28 ESV), and I am holding on to that promise.

**LORD**, I choose to worship You in these times when I can't sleep. For there is no better way to spend my time. I will sing to You and speak praises to You! I will bask in Your compassion, Your calm, Your company!

**"SOVEREIGN LORD**, you have made the heavens and the earth by your great power and outstretched arm. Nothing is too hard for you" (Jeremiah 32:17 NIV). Surely helping me get some sleep is not too hard for You either. I trust that You will provide for me the rest that I need.

# LOSS OF A JOB

*"For I know the plans I have for you, declares
the Lord, plans for welfare and not for
evil, to give you a future and a hope."*
JEREMIAH 29:11 ESV

---

Sometimes we can see the writing on the wall and sometimes we're just blindsided, but regardless of the reason, losing a job can be a crushing blow—and not just to our finances but to our mental health too. Anxieties, worries, and fears abound in times of job loss. And then there's the stress found during the search process for new work, in addition to the pressure in the first days of a new position once it's found. But God is faithful. He will provide the job we need to give us the money to buy all the things we need. And throughout the losing, looking, and landing process, we must remember nothing that happens to us can ever spoil or alter the perfect plans God has for us.

**LORD**, I'm devastated. I needed my job. This layoff has blindsided me. I'm so upset that I can't think straight about how to move forward. Please clear my head. Help me to focus on the blessings in the moment and trust You will provide for my future.

**FATHER**, You've helped me through big changes in the past. Remind me of Your care and provision, then help me experience peace and gain the confidence that You will carry me through the coming days. I have no reason to doubt You and every reason to trust You.

**DEAR GOD**, I'm grieving because I loved my job. To me it wasn't just a paycheck—it was meaningful, and I will miss it. If money were no issue, I would have done the job without pay, that's how much I enjoyed it. And I'll miss so many of the people with whom I worked day after day. As I grieve, please help me to trust that in time You will fill up my life with joy and satisfaction in new ways. You created me with good plans in mind, and so I trust that this job loss is part of Your plan that there is a new place or position where You want and need me to be.

**LORD**, You give and take away, but still I always want to say, "Blessed be Your name" (Job 1:21).

**LORD**, You have said, "Do not remember the things that have happened before. Do not think about the things of the past. See, I will do a new thing. It will begin happening now. Will you not know about it? I will even make a road in the wilderness, and rivers in the desert" (Isaiah 43:18–19 NLV). I trust You to do a new thing in my life now. I believe You will perform miracles in this situation, just like You make roads in the wilderness and rivers in the desert. You are amazing, God! I could not get through this without You, and I know You will bring me through victorious!

**GOD**, please help me to manage my finances well, especially in this uncertain time between jobs. Help me to make wise adjustments in spending where possible, but also help me to never stop being generous to give back to You and those in need in Your name.

**FATHER**, You connect people like no one else can. Please lead me to the people in my church and community who can help me find a new job. I pray that You would let my résumés and applications get into the hands of exactly the right people, at exactly the right place, at exactly the right time.

Please show me if there are skills that I have that I've not been using or new skills You want me to learn, Father. Direct me if You want me to further my education during this time and show me how I can afford it.

When I'm growing tired and discouraged and weary of job hunting, Lord, please refresh and renew me. Help me to trust in Your perfect timing. Help me to be filled with excitement and confidence for the new doors You are going to open at exactly the right time.

# LOSS OF A LOVED ONE

*Blessed are they that mourn:*
*for they shall be comforted.*
MATTHEW 5:4 KJV

Jesus knows and cares about our grief. He became human just like we are human, and He understands what it's like to lose a precious loved one. Since we know God is sovereign, it can be so hard to understand why He allows us to suffer through the deep pain, sorrow, and loneliness of grief. But we have a choice to turn from Him in bitterness and anger or run to Him and let Him comfort and heal us—and give us greater confidence in our hope that He alone offers us eternal life because of Jesus Christ's work on the cross; and that although we may be weeping during our night of grief, one day our joy will come with the morning light (Psalm 30:5).

**OH, GOD,** I am so broken. I have never felt pain like this or felt such an empty place in my life. I loved her so much, I need her so much, and now she is gone? I can't seem to wrap my head around that reality. Hold me close, Lord, and may Your Spirit intercede for me, as I don't know what else to pray.

**GOD**, I'm desperate for understanding. *Why, how* could this happen? I can't fathom it. How do I go on? I feel like I'm only able to function at all because You are sustaining me. And for that I thank You!

**FATHER**, I'm so hurt and angry because I know You could have healed my loved one and stopped this from ever happening. Why? You can work miracles. You could have shown Your healing power, and what a testimony that would have been! I'm so confused and lost. But I also desperately don't want my anger to harden my heart and make me grow bitter toward You. So I pray You would keep me close, Lord, even though I don't understand. Pull me back toward You when I try to pull away. Surround me with Your tangible love and truth in so many ways, through so many people.

**LORD**, grieving the loss of my loved one is such a roller-coaster ride. One moment I'm up and dealing okay, trusting in You and feeling some peace. The next, I'm down in anger and fear and total despair again. I pray the ride smooths out eventually. Please let it be so.

**FATHER**, I believe that "You keep track of all my sorrows. You have collected all my tears in your bottle. You have recorded each one in your book" (Psalm 56:8 NLT). It must be a huge bottle and book You have, Lord, because I have cried so many tears. Thank You that You care so much, for loving me as much as You do, so much more than anyone else.

**FATHER**, surround me with people who understand deep loss, grief, and pain such as I am experiencing now, in this moment. Help me to bond and connect with the people You want to use to comfort and guide me. I'm trusting that You have comforted them so that they can comfort me, and that one day I can continue this good work by passing on to others the blessings of comfort I have received as well (2 Corinthians 1:3–5).

**LORD**, let all of us who loved the precious person who is gone now come together and honor a life well lived and celebrate and share the memories we all have with joy and gratitude, even if it's bittersweet to do so. Help us to grieve well together and comfort one another.

**FATHER**, please shield and protect me from coping in unhealthy ways as I grieve for the loss of my loved one. I can empathize in a new and horrible way about why some people turn to alcohol and drugs and all kinds of sinful choices to cope. The pain of losing a close and precious loved one is just so intense, and the enemy takes that opportunity to attack and tempt with ways that might seem to ease the pain for a short time but will eventually destroy me. Guard me, Almighty God! Send Your angels to meet me.

**JESUS,** You said, "I am the resurrection and the life. Whoever believes in me, though he die, yet shall he live" (John 11:25 ESV). I am so extremely grateful that my loved one I just lost trusted in You as Savior from sin. I believe that he is alive again, just as You promised. That I will see him again and we will spend eternity together because our hope and trust is in You. Please work Your good plans through my grief. Help me to be extra motivated to share the gospel with others so that more people will come to find salvation and have eternal life in You.

# LOSS OF A PET

*"Are not five sparrows sold for two pennies?*
*Yet not one of them is forgotten by God."*
LUKE 12:6 NIV

---

Our awesome Creator God blessed this world with amazing animals, and those of us who love our pets dearly know how deeply painful it is to lose them. While our interactions with our animal companions is not the same as human relationships, our pets do provide their own kind of sweet friendship and love in our lives. They are full of joy and fun and provide entertainment. They are generally easy to please and care for, and we receive a deep, devoted love and loyalty in return. We come to depend on their comforting companionship through all kinds of ups and downs and stresses of life. And so losing them brings a sense of insecurity and uncertainty, leaving a hole that seems unfillable. Do we want a new pet or not? And when is the timing right? How can we ever go through this loss again? Each pet is one of a kind, so how will we ever stop missing them? Fortunately, our God who has even every hair of our heads numbered (Luke 12:7) cares much about us and our love of His creatures. He will comfort, bless, provide, and guide us through our days of loss.

**FATHER**, I'm heartbroken. My pet was so precious to me, such a beloved part of my family, a loyal friend and companion. I knew when he came into my life that he could not live forever and someday he would leave my life, but still it hurts that this is now my reality. I pray for an outpouring of Your comfort in this time of loss.

**LORD GOD**, I long for the day when death is swallowed up forever and You wipe away tears from all faces (Isaiah 25:8), even death of our beloved pets and the tears we cry for them. Until that day arrives, I pray You would give me the fortitude to go on.

**LORD**, the house is too quiet without my pet. It seems unbelievable that she is gone. I keep absentmindedly looking for her and expecting her to be near me. I long to pet her and feel the comfort of her snuggled in my lap. I am just so sad and miss her so much. Please comfort me, Lord.

**CREATOR GOD**, thank You for the gift of animals and pets in this world. Your creativity is amazing, and Your compassion is unmatched. You knew we humans would need the extra special love and loyalty that pets give us in our lives. Help me to focus on gratitude for the time I had with my dear pet and gratitude to You for letting me experience this blessing.

**FATHER**, thank You for teaching me more about unconditional love through my pet. If a created animal can love me like that, how much more do You, the Creator, love me? I am so looking forward to eternity with You when all sorrows are eliminated, and there is only joy and peace and love forever.

Help me to continue to delight in the gift of animals, even while I grieve the loss of my dear pet. Animals give such comfort and joy and are a testimony of Your awesomeness and creativity, God! They are such a blessing from You.

# MARRIAGE STRESS

*Above all, love each other deeply,*
*because love covers over a multitude of sins.*
1 PETER 4:8 NIV

---

The vows we make on our wedding day seem like the easiest-ever promises to make. The deep love for each other and the excitement we feel to start a new life together eclipse any thought of the trials of our relationship that may come. This kind of love will get us through anything, we think. But as the years pass, we realize that love and those vows are tested, big-time, because we are human. We are inherently selfish. Our first instinct is to look after our own interests, yet marriage is a constant challenge to be intentional to follow the words of the apostle Paul when he said, "Do nothing out of selfish ambition or vain conceit. Rather, in humility value others above yourselves, not looking to your own interests but each of you to the interests of the others" (Philippians 2:3–4 NIV). During the times of trial and testing of our relationship, may we look to God to help us honor the vows we have made to our spouse and follow His good commands for marriage—and then experience His great blessings for doing so.

**LORD**, thank You for the wonderful blessing of my marriage. Even though it can be stressful sometimes, it truly is such a gift. When we feel out of sorts and angry with each other, remind us of the love and excitement that first drew us together. Help us to rekindle our romance every day.

**GOD**, You said, "It is not good that the man should be alone; I will make him a helper fit for him" (Genesis 2:18 ESV). There is purpose and goodness in Your order and intentions when You created man and woman. I thank You that I am my husband's helper and he is mine. Let us be a good team. Let us understand each other's strengths and weaknesses with appreciation and grace.

We have hit a rough patch, Lord, and we desperately need good communication and grace for each other. Help us to listen to one another with love. Help us to be "quick to hear, slow to speak, slow to anger" (James 1:19 esv). May we listen with intent and speak knowing the power of our words. May we look to heal instead of hurt.

Marriage definitely tests our willingness to forgive, Lord. Don't let us forget Your extraordinary grace and the way You forgive us. Help us remember that we are to forgive not just "seven times but seventy times seven" (Matthew 18:22 nlv)!

I'm very frightened about what's happening in my marriage, Father. I don't understand how we've gotten to this point. I'm not even sure how to pray. Please help us fix what's broken. Show us our sin and help us confess to one another and reconcile our differences. Show us the grace, forgiveness, and mending we need to do. Then help us find joy, passion, and a deeper love in the making up.

Stresses of life and work and family can make a husband and wife start to grow apart before they even realize what's happening, Lord! Help us to be very intentional about protecting and nurturing our marriage.

Your Word says at the very beginning, God, that "a man shall leave his father and his mother and hold fast to his wife, and they shall become one flesh" (Genesis 2:24 ESV). Thank You for oneness with my husband, God. It is such a sacred union designed by You. No wonder the enemy is constantly trying to destroy marriages. Please help us to respect, honor, and protect our union and encourage other husbands and wives to do the same.

**LORD**, help us submit "to one another out of reverence for Christ" (Ephesians 5:21 ESV). Help us to learn and obey all the good instructions for marriage that You have given us in Your Word.

**JESUS**, for those who are believers married to spouses who do not believe in You, I thank You for Your instruction in Your Word, especially in 1 Corinthians 7. Help them to understand and follow it well. May unbelieving spouses eventually come to salvation in You because they've been given much patience and love.

**GOD**, what You have joined together, let no one else separate (Mark 10:9)! I pray for Your protection of my marriage.

# MOVING

*Trust in the Lord, and do good. So you will live in
the land and will be fed. Be happy in the Lord. And
He will give you the desires of your heart. Give your
way over to the Lord. Trust in Him also. And He will
do it. He will make your being right and good show
as the light, and your wise actions as the noon day.*

PSALM 37:3–6 NLV

---

Making a move can be one of the most stressful
times of life. It's amazing what we can accumulate
in even a short amount of time in our homes. Not to
mention if you've spent years and years in one place.
But even harder to deal with when moving is to leave
the people you've developed community with. On the
flip side, maybe the opportunity to purge unneeded
items and become more minimalistic is appealing.
And maybe what has prompted the move is a need
for new community and new connections. Whatever
the motivations and emotions involved in a move,
it is an uncertain time in so many ways as we navigate
the details, say goodbye to the old and hello to the
new, and then start to settle in. May we, through
the process of the coming and the going, remember
that God is our constant source of stability and peace,
in any home, at any time, in any place.

**FATHER**, I'm both excited and nervous, happy and scared. This big move will be a new adventure for sure. I am so sad to say goodbye to many things but also eager to say hello to new people, places, and experiences. Knowing You will be my steady rock through it all is a great comfort for me and my family. Thank You!

**GOD**, You alone are my rock and my salvation and my fortress. You are the one who saves me. You are my strong place. Because of Your presence in my life and Your Word in my heart, I shall not be shaken (Psalm 62:6 ESV).

**LORD**, I believe You are the Creator and Giver of life and breath, and You set the times and places for people to live (Acts 17:24–26). I have sensed You leading me to make this move and live in this new place for this upcoming season of life. Please continue to guide and direct me.

Moving can be so stressful, God! Please show us Your love in many little details as my family makes this move. Let the logistics work out smoothly. Help us to be organized and efficient in packing up and then unpacking in our new home. Let our new neighbors be kind, friendly, and full of grace. As we notice each little blessing, we want to thank and praise You for it. Please grow our faith and gratitude through this moving experience.

**FATHER**, please comfort the ones who love us and will miss us because of this move. Comfort our hearts too, over missing them back. Help us to be able to maintain our friendship across the miles. And please bring us all new opportunities and new friendships to fill the empty places in our hearts.

**JESUS**, no matter where I move or how many times I do so, I'm so thankful for the heavenly home that You are preparing, the one that I can look forward to forever (John 14:1–6). Thank You for being my Savior from sin so that I can spend eternity with You and all those that hope and believe in You!

# PANDEMICS

*[Jesus] added, "Nation will go to war against nation,*
*and kingdom against kingdom. There will be great*
*earthquakes, and there will be famines and plagues in*
*many lands, and there will be terrifying things and*
*great miraculous signs from heaven. But before all this*
*occurs, there will be a time of great persecution. You*
*will be dragged into synagogues and prisons, and you*
*will stand trial before kings and governors because you*
*are my followers. But this will be your opportunity*
*to tell them about me. So don't worry in advance*
*about how to answer the charges against you, for I*
*will give you the right words and such wisdom that*
*none of your opponents will be able to reply or refute*
*you! Even those closest to you—your parents, brothers,*
*relatives, and friends—will betray you. They will even*
*kill some of you. And everyone will hate you because*
*you are my followers. But not a hair of your head will*
*perish! By standing firm, you will win your souls."*

LUKE 21:10–19 NLT

---

It's amazing and awful the amount of fear, chaos, destruction, and distress an invisible virus can inflict on the world. Yet pandemics and other world tragedies and calamities shouldn't surprise us as Christians. Jesus told us to expect them. But He also told us to stand firm in our faith. He promises to protect us and give us victory over it all, as we proclaim His love and truth amid any hardship and the uncertainties it may bring.

**LORD**, comfort all the grieving who have lost loved ones during this pandemic. You see and know the pain. Show me the ways I can bless and help them. Show me what part I can play—little or big—to ease the suffering of others.

**FATHER**, health-care workers and first responders definitely need supernatural strength and stamina during these chaotic days with an unpredictable and deadly virus on the loose. They are true heroes. Please bless them abundantly.

**FATHER**, it's so awful to feel afraid of something invisible and unpredictable. I can do my best to not catch this virus, but my best might not be enough. Remind me of Your sovereignty, Father. Remind me that all the days of my life were written in Your book before one of them came to be (Psalm 139:16). I don't want to be reckless and foolish, but I also don't want to live in fear. Help me to find the right balance and live according to Your will and perfect plans for my life.

**LORD**, show us the wise ways to help protect ourselves, our family, our friends, and our neighbors during this pandemic. But help us to consider *whole* health. Total isolation is not the answer, since our mental health matters too, and You have designed us for community. Give us wisdom, understanding, and grace as we make our way through these uncertain days.

**GOD**, I know Satan wants to lie to me, to keep me in fear and paralyze me from doing any good works in Your name, to share Your love and truth. Help me to fight the lies and fear and listen to You, Lord!

**"O LORD MY GOD**, I cried to you for help, and you have healed me" (Psalm 30:2 ESV). I thank and praise You for protecting me from death and healing me from this virus and restoring me to full health! Show me the ways I can serve You and care for others in Your name again now that I am well.

# PRODIGAL CHILDREN

*"When he finally came to his senses, he said to himself,
'At home even the hired servants have food enough
to spare, and here I am dying of hunger! I will go
home to my father and say, "Father, I have sinned
against both heaven and you, and I am no longer
worthy of being called your son. Please take me on as
a hired servant."' So he returned home to his father.
And while he was still a long way off, his father
saw him coming. Filled with love and compassion,
he ran to his son, embraced him, and kissed him."*

LUKE 15:17–20 NLT

As parents we'd rather take on any pain than have our child go through it, and so to watch a child willfully go astray and cause his own pain brings us extraordinary heartache. We long to run to his rescue the way we did when he was little—but he has purposely gone far beyond our protection. Yet even when our children were babies, they were never truly ours. They always belonged first and foremost to our heavenly Father. And they still do. So as hard as it is for us to sit back and wait, we can entrust them to God's love as we constantly pray. In the midst of what looks to us like chaos and confusion, He is able to protect them and lead them into peace, blessing, and reconciliation once again.

**OH LORD**, my heart is constantly aching over my prodigal child. I can't believe this is my reality. We were once so close. I am his earthly parent, but You are his heavenly Father. You love him even more than I do. You see him now, and You know all. Your perspective is so far beyond mine. Please shield and protect my prodigal son and draw him back to us, I beg You!

Teach me what You want me to learn through this experience and pain, Father. Help me to connect with other mothers of prodigal children so that we can empathize, encourage, and pray for one another.

**LORD**, I know my prodigal child thinks that since she is so wrapped up in sin anyway, it doesn't matter if she keeps on living and reveling in it. Show her that it does indeed matter. Let her see sin's destructive consequences so that she'll want to turn around to You. Most of all, show her that we are all sinners and if we confess our sins, You are faithful and just to forgive us and to cleanse us from all unrighteousness (1 John 1:9). I praise You for that! And for the fact that You take our sins away as far as the east is from the west (Psalm 103:12). Please help my prodigal child understand these truths.

Only You are the perfect parent, heavenly Father. I'm definitely not! I'm far from it, and that's something that I'm not proud of. Please forgive me of all my mistakes as a parent. If there is something specific and hurtful I've done that my prodigal child is holding against me, please help him to want to communicate with me so that I can ask forgiveness and we can reconcile.

**LORD**, I beg You to intervene in this situation, and I need great patience until my prodigal child turns around. I will wait for You and be strong. I will let my heart take courage as I wait for You to move (Psalm 27:14).

**LORD**, I feel so helpless and scared for my child. Where is she right now? Is she safe? Is anyone hurting or abusing her? I could go crazy with anxiety for her, if not for Your unexplainable peace. Please keep filling me with it, Lord. It's miraculously sustaining me. I can only pray for You to keep watch over my prodigal child. She has her own free will, but I desperately pray that she chooses to turn around, to turn to You.

**LORD**, Your Word says, "Train up a child in the way he should go; even when he is old he will not depart from it" (Proverbs 22:6 ESV). I feel like I did my best to train my child well, but I know I made mistakes. Please cover those mistakes with Your grace, Lord! And let my child have a change of heart and mind. Let me see that in the end he won't depart from good training but will come back to me and You.

# STRESS AT WORK

*"Come to me, all who labor and are heavy laden,
and I will give you rest. Take my yoke upon you,
and learn from me, for I am gentle and lowly
in heart, and you will find rest for your souls.
For my yoke is easy, and my burden is light."*

Matthew 11:28–30 esv

Loads of responsibilities, tight deadlines, conflicts with coworkers and supervisors—all these kinds of things can cause us so much stress at work. And if we're unsure when we will ever have a true break from it all, we can soon suffer from total burnout. We spend a good amount of time and energy in our lives at our workplaces though, so we need to be able to find joy and satisfaction there, not just stress and tension. Whether that means a job change or just finding new ways to keep a good work/personal life balance, we must not forget God's presence with us in every moment. Even on our busiest, most anxious days on the job, we must take time for prayer and remember to depend on His constant love and care.

**LORD**, how can I ever get all these projects done on time? My boss must think I'm a superhero or can work all day every day and all night too. You know I'm not being lazy or irresponsible. Help me to bear what I can of this load right now, and then please give me courage to have an open dialogue with my boss so that we might figure out more manageable workloads for me as soon as possible. I can't go on like this much longer. Please allow my boss to be gracious toward me. Help him to listen well and be understanding as we work together toward a good solution.

I commit my way to You, Lord. I trust in You and I believe You will act (Psalm 37:5) on my behalf in this stressful situation.

**FATHER,** a particular coworker of mine is so difficult to work with. You know who I mean. His attitudes and work ethic are so frustrating. Please give me the wisdom and patience to get along with him. Please give him more wisdom and maturity. Help me to have opportunities to talk with him about You and the gospel, Lord. If he does not yet know You, I pray You would open his eyes to You, his Savior.

**LORD,** I'm thankful for my job and the money that I can earn, but I've just grown so bored with my current position. Please show me if I should move on to something else or stay where I am. Please open doors of opportunity for me wherever I am so that I can use the gifts You have given me in new ways.

**GOD**, this deadline is looming, and nothing seems to be going right with this project. Please give me renewed energy and creativity. I praise and thank You for my abilities. May I and my work bring glory to You!

**FATHER**, my upcoming vacation cannot come soon enough. I feel like I've been near total burnout. I pray my days away will be a truly restful time. I pray this break will reenergize me and help me return to work with a new attitude and a renewed sense of purpose. Thank You for the blessing of vacation time!

**GOD**, You are my refuge and strength, "a very present help in trouble" (Psalm 46:1 ESV). I love that phrase. You're not just up there unreachable in the sky. You are right here beside me, giving me strength and peace, because of Your Holy Spirit. You are with me through every stressful moment of my workday and every other moment too. Thank You for staying close, for loving me, for Your calm amid chaos.

**JESUS**, help me to shine Your light upon my coworkers. Give me many opportunities to be kind to them and to share Your good news with them. May they come to a saving faith in You!

**LORD**, I'm having physical symptoms like headaches and heartburn because of stress at work. Please help the stressful issues to calm down and resolve themselves. Help me remember to take better care of myself with good nutrition and to take time for both exercise and relaxation. Help me tap into the unsurpassable peace I can only attain through You.

Just a little encouragement can go such a long way, Lord! Please help my boss to share good words and positive feedback instead of just criticism. Help me to encourage anyone I can at work too.

I'm grieving a bit as I leave this job, Lord, but it was my choice and You opened a new door. Yet I will miss many things here, including many coworkers. Please bless this place and these people.

I'm starting this new job, and I'm so nervous, God! Please calm my anxieties and fear. Help me to acclimate quickly and smoothly. I pray for positive and helpful coworkers who will give me grace as I learn the ropes. Thank You for this opportunity and for the perfect plan You have for my work and life.

# SURGERY

*When I am afraid, I put my trust in you.*
Psalm 56:3 esv

Facing a medical procedure or surgery can fill us with great anxiety and fear. With a looming date and time to be at the hospital, we cannot deny that we don't control our lives. We must trust in the care of doctors and medical professionals, and mostly in God's care. We go under anesthesia, uncertain what we will find when we wake up. But through it all, God never leaves us. He fills us with His presence. He loves us and keeps us. He serves as our refuge, our strength, and our protector. He will guide the doctors' and nurses' minds, hands, and feet to help heal us, and He will work out the good plans He has for our lives, both here on earth and in heaven.

**LORD**, I'm beyond nervous for this surgery. I have so many questions. What will I feel like when I wake up? Will I come out of the anesthesia okay? How much pain will I have? Will the pain medication be effective? What if I have a reaction to it? What will my recovery time be? Will I need physical therapy? Please clear these questions from my mind. It doesn't do any good to fret over them. I trust my life to You, Lord. With You hovering over me, standing beside me, and residing within me, I have nothing to fear.

**FATHER GOD**, I'll be picturing You standing right beside my hospital bed as they roll me back to surgery saying, "Don't be afraid, for I am with you. Don't be discouraged, for I am your God. I will strengthen you and help you. I will hold you up with my victorious right hand" (Isaiah 41:10 NLT).

**GOD**, I want to focus on gratitude instead of worry. I'm grateful for good doctors, surgeons, nurses, and all the staff. I'm grateful for modern medicine and anesthesia. I'm grateful for pain medication. I'm grateful for health insurance and payment programs to cover the cost. I'm grateful I learned of the need for this surgery before this condition might have killed me. I'm grateful for my family and friends supporting and helping me through this.

**LORD**, when this surgery is over, I want to say, "I sought the LORD, and he answered me and delivered me from all my fears" (Psalm 34:4 ESV). I'm trusting that will be true.

**LORD**, I trust the outcome of this surgery to You. Please guide the anesthesiologist. Please guide the surgeon's hands. Please guide all the nurses and staff who will care for me today. Please work through them to bring healing to my body.

Throughout this surgery process, Lord, let me find ways to share Your love and kindness with the people who care for me. Help me to stay positive and grateful and encouraging to the medical staff and my loved ones supporting me. Despite my circumstances, give me a merry heart and let me show all of those around me how such a heart does good like medicine, as Your Word promises (Proverbs 17:22).

**DEAR GOD**, I'm worried about strong pain medication. I hear so many scary stories of people becoming addicted to it. Please help the pain not be too bad after surgery, and help me to manage it wisely.

**LORD**, "even though I walk through the valley of the shadow of death, I will fear no evil, for you are with me; your rod and your staff, they comfort me" (Psalm 23:4 ESV). You and Your peace, You and Your presence are all I need to see me through.

**FATHER,** when this surgery is over, please help me to get much more serious about getting my health back on track as best I can. Give me the wisdom to choose mostly good-for-me foods, to exercise regularly, to look for ways to eliminate unnecessary stress. And may I find more calm by spending more time in the peace of Your presence.

**LORD,** I'm so grateful for the family and friends You've given me to support me and walk with me before and after this surgery. Please remind me to let them know how much I appreciate them.

# UNSTABLE PREGNANCY

*You watched me as I was being formed in utter seclusion, as I was woven together in the dark of the womb. You saw me before I was born. Every day of my life was recorded in your book. Every moment was laid out before a single day had passed.*

PSALM 139:15–16 NLT

Oh, the sweet, mysterious joy of a mother carrying a precious baby inside her womb! But when something goes wrong and the baby's health and life are in danger, the fear, anxiety, and uncertainty can be crippling. But we must trust in God, remembering that He alone numbers our days and the days of our children. Only He knows the outcome of the new lives He weaves together in a mother's womb. Rest assured that even the tiniest unborn baby is known and seen by Him—and every day of his or her precious life, whether in utero, on earth, or in heaven is counted by Him and matters to Him. Every life is precious.

**OH, FATHER,** I'm so scared because the doctors have said there is a good chance I could lose this dear baby. Please don't let that happen. Work a miracle in our lives. Help me to stay calm. For I know that anxiety in my mind and body will only put the baby more at risk. Lord, fill me with Your peace that "transcends all understanding" (Philippians 4:7 NIV).

**LORD,** I want to obey the doctors exactly to help give my baby every chance at life and good health. Help me to endure these months of mostly bed rest that they have prescribed. It sure gives me a lot of time for reading Your Word and talking to You in prayer. I'm grateful for that. Draw me closer to You during these difficult days. Please bless me and this precious child growing within me.

**GOD**, You told the prophet Jeremiah, "I knew you before I formed you in your mother's womb" (Jeremiah 1:5 NLT). You know all things, and I believe You knew the baby who is now in my womb before You formed him or her there. I believe You love and care about my baby, and he or she was not formed by accident. You have a plan for his or her life, as well as mine. I don't know what that plan is, but You do, Lord. And it is in You I trust!

**JESUS**, You said, "A woman giving birth to a child has pain because her time has come; but when her baby is born she forgets the anguish because of her joy that a child is born into the world" (John 16:21 NIV). Please help me make it to full-term with this dear baby and let me experience the pain and anguish of labor and delivery, and then the extreme joy that follows upon her entrance into this world.

# WARS AND RUMORS OF WARS

*As Jesus was sitting on the Mount of Olives, the disciples came to him privately. "Tell us," they said, "when will this happen, and what will be the sign of your coming and of the end of the age?" Jesus answered: "Watch out that no one deceives you. For many will come in my name, claiming, 'I am the Messiah,' and will deceive many. You will hear of wars and rumors of wars, but see to it that you are not alarmed. Such things must happen, but the end is still to come. Nation will rise against nation, and kingdom against kingdom. There will be famines and earthquakes in various places. All these are the beginning of birth pains."*

MATTHEW 24:3–8 NIV

---

The news need not surprise us when we "hear of wars and rumors of wars." Jesus called it long ago when the disciples asked what sign to look for of the coming of the end of the age and Jesus' return. "But see to it that you are not alarmed," He assured them. Yes, it all sounds quite scary, but everyone who stands firm to the end, keeping faith in Jesus and God's sovereignty, will be saved.

**JESUS**, it's hard not to be alarmed. The news makes everything sound so scary. Even when wars and rumors of wars are far away across the world, they feel close somehow because of the way we are all so connected through Internet communication these days. Give me peace in knowing that You predicted all of this. You are not scared or surprised. You are victorious in all ways, and I am Yours. You will guard and guide me to the very end. You are my salvation.

**GOD**, You have not given me a spirit of fear but rather a spirit "of power, and of love, and of a sound mind" (2 Timothy 1:7 kjv). No matter what is going on in the world, help me to be courageous and loving and full of Your wisdom.

**HEAVENLY FATHER**, watch over all the innocent civilians and refugees and especially the children affected by wars and rumors of wars. Protect them and show them Your care. Thank You for the ministries and people loving and serving in Your name. May Your kingdom grow as the good news is shared. Show me the specific things You want me to do to help and contribute.

**JESUS**, I pray for people fighting on both sides of war, the ordinary people caught up in the evils of this world. Show those who are lost in sin and in want of a Savior their need of You, Jesus. Let them hear the gospel and believe in You to save them.

**LORD**, Your armor is the best thing to equip me so that I will be ready for anything. I am standing firm with the belt of truth buckled around my waist, the breastplate of righteousness in place, and with my feet fitted with the readiness that comes from the gospel of peace. I take up the shield of faith, so that I can extinguish all the flaming arrows of the evil one. And I take up the helmet of salvation and the sword of the Spirit, which is the Word of God (Ephesians 6:14–17 NIV).

**GOD**, You offer real hope and salvation to everyone of every nation. You so loved the world that You gave Your only Son, Jesus, "that whoever believes in Him should not perish but have eternal life" (John 3:16). He alone is the Way, Truth, and Life (John 14:6). Hallelujah!

# WEAKNESS

*I was given a thorn in my flesh, a messenger of Satan, to torment me. Three times I pleaded with the Lord to take it away from me. But he said to me, "My grace is sufficient for you, for my power is made perfect in weakness." Therefore I will boast all the more gladly about my weaknesses, so that Christ's power may rest on me. That is why, for Christ's sake, I delight in weaknesses, in insults, in hardships, in persecutions, in difficulties. For when I am weak, then I am strong.*

2 Corinthians 12:7–10 niv

Feeling weak in any situation might make us worry and fret, but we don't need to. God's Word shows us that we should actually boast gladly about our human weaknesses because they give us the opportunity to rely fully on the strength and power of Jesus. When we know we are totally incapable of handling something on our own, we depend desperately on Jesus—and there's no better thing we can do.

**GOD**, when I'm feeling so weak and helpless that I don't even know what to pray, remind me that the Holy Spirit is praying to You on my behalf, that the Spirit helps me in my weakness (Romans 8:26). What a blessing!

**JESUS**, remind me that You can sympathize with my weaknesses. You know what it's like to be human. You were tempted in all the ways I am, but You were without sin, and so You provide the way for me to come to God's throne and receive mercy and grace whenever I need it (Hebrews 4:15–16). I don't deserve Your amazing love, Jesus, but I'm so thankful for it.

**LORD**, You are my strength and my song. You are my salvation. I praise and exalt You (Exodus 15:2)!

**GOD**, help me to learn from the stories of faith of people like "Gideon, Barak, Samson, Jephthah, David, Samuel, and all the prophets. By faith these people overthrew kingdoms, ruled with justice, and received what God had promised them. They shut the mouths of lions, quenched the flames of fire, and escaped death by the edge of the sword. Their weakness was turned to strength. They became strong in battle and put whole armies to flight" (Hebrews 11:32–34 NLT).

**GOD**, I ask You to "give justice to the poor and the orphan; uphold the rights of the oppressed and the destitute. Rescue the poor and helpless; deliver them from the grasp of evil people" (Psalm 82:3–4 NLT).

**LORD**, You are my helper; I will not fear. What can any person do to me (Hebrews 13:6 ESV) when You stand by my side?

**ALMIGHTY GOD**, I sure don't have the strength on my own, but I can do all things through You because You strengthen me (Philippians 4:13)!

# ABOUT THE AUTHOR

JoAnne Simmons is a writer and editor who's in awe of God's love and the ways He guides and provides. Her favorite things include coffee shops, libraries, the Bible, good grammar, being a wife and mom, dogs, music, punctuation, church, the beach, and many dear family and friends—but not in that order. If her family weren't so loving and flexible, she'd be in big trouble; and if God's mercies weren't new every morning, she'd never get out of bed.